ABA –A Brief Introduction to Teaching Children with Autism

ABA – A Brief Introduction to Teaching Children with Autism

Reg Reynolds, Ph.D., C.Psych.

Lulu Enterprises, Inc. • 2010

Published by Lulu Enterprises, Inc.: www.lulu.com

ISBN 978-0-557-84591-0

*To Joyce, the love of my life,
who has put up with my obsessions for almost sixty
years; to my daughter, Alison, who got me interested
in teaching children with autism; and with
appreciation to Dr. Janis Williams, C.Psych.,
who has been kind enough to encourage
my interest in this field.*

Preface

This book was written as a white paper expressing my opinion regarding the use of ABA in the teaching of children with autism, and updated over a period of years for the direction of the Senior Therapists with whom I was working at the time. It is being published now so that the information which it contains can be more readily available.

I believe that it can be of significant help to the parents of the many children being diagnosed with autism, as well as the professionals who work with them. This is where I think they should start.

In this manuscript, I have tried to incorporate the wisdom of all with whom I have come in contact, hopefully giving credit to the many sources from which the ideas in this book have been drawn. I particularly wish to acknowledge the generosity of Drs. Vincent Carbone and Richard Solomon in freely sharing with me from their own areas of expertise.

Finally, if I have inadvertantly failed to acknowledge the source of any of the ideas in this publication, I sincerely apologize.

Table of Contents

Introduction

I am not an ABA person per sē. Although originally trained as a teacher, my background is primarily in clinical psychology and, although I began my psychology career by working with children, I have only returned to working with that population within the past nine or ten years, after many years of working with adults. The opinions expressed in this presentation represent my "take" on teaching children with autism; they are only that – my opinions on the subject.[1] On the other hand, this is an area of particular interest to me, and my former job[2] has provided me with the opportunity to observe many excellent ABA service providers in action.

I would like to acknowledge the inspiration that I have received from Vince Carbone (charismatic proponent of what has come to be known as the Verbal Behaviour approach to ABA), Marcie Norton (who first showed me that ABA could be both intense and fun), Diane Sardi (my guide to good, standard ABA practices), Sandy Palombo (for thinking outside the traditional ABA box), and John DeMarco (who is certified in both ABA and RDI).

I would strongly urge parents of children with autism to learn the teaching strategies discussed in the following pages and apply them in all their interactions with their child, for a number of reasons:

First, experience has shown that a child's progress in ABA is directly related to the extent to which his or her parents are involved in his or her teaching/training – if the parents happen to be fortunate enough to be able to hire an experienced Clinical Supervisor for their child's program, they should insist that they be taught to use the same effective teaching procedures that are used by ABA Instructor

---

[1] This document represents my thoughts on the subject as of December 2010.

[2] As Supervising Clinician with ErinoakKids, the agency responsible for administering the Ontario Government's Intensive Behavioural Intervention program for children with autism in the Central West Region of the province, from 2001 to 2009.

Therapists, and that they be as involved in their child's ABA program as they are able to be. Sources of training, in addition to that provided directly by the Service Provider/Clinical Supervisor and the Senior Therapist include:

The Verbal Behavior Approach by Mary Lynch Barbera (2007),

Educate Toward Recovery by Robert Schramm (2006).

Training Videos and CD's (such as Vince Carbone's 7 CD set of videos, "The Verbal Behavior Approach to Teaching Children with Autism").

The Training Manual (and Program Manager's Guide) from Kathy Lear's Help Us Learn books.

The Mariposa School's Employee Training Manual (for Verbal Behaviour), which you can download from their website at www.MariposaSchool.org

Christina Burk's website (www.ChristinaBurkABA.com), particularly for the section on *Effective Teaching Procedures.*

The Certified Behavior Analyst Learning Module series (from Behavior Development Solutions, telephone 203 263-0892)

www.verbalbehaviornetwork.com

Various university and community college ABA courses.

The material presented in many available workshops.

Second, there are many opportunities for teaching/learning outside of any formal instruction program which may be set up for the child, and most of that teaching has to be done by the parents. Some years ago there was a book about psychotherapy called "The Other Twenty-Three Hours." Its point was that what goes on during the rest of the day is just as important, and possibly even more important, than what goes on during the psychotherapy hour. The same principle applies to a child's ABA program. Regardless of how intensive it may be, there is going to be a lot of "dead time" unless the parents can learn how to apply ABA principles throughout the child's waking hours.

Third, because ABA for children with autism is most often provided within the context of intensive behavioural intervention (IBI), and because this is expensive and outside funding is usually limited, parents should learn how to provide the instruction that their child is likely to need on an ongoing basis for many years to come. One way to begin this learning process might be for each of the parents to provide some of the formal instruction under the guidance of a Senior Therapist, being trained in ABA procedures just as if they were intending to be Instructor Therapists – perhaps as much as one session per week – and have their application of the procedures that they are learning generalized to the child's natural environment under the supervision of the Senior Therapist and/or one of the more experienced Instructor Therapists.

Autism and Pervasive Developmental Disorders (from DSM IV)

- Autism Spectrum Disorders[3]
  - Autism
  - Asperger's Disorder
  - PDD - NOS (PDD - Not Otherwise Specified)
- Rett's Disorder (an X chromosome mutation only observed in girls, Rett's Disorder is characterized by neurological regression, mid-line hand-wringing movements, seizures)
- Childhood Disintegrative Disorder (a very rare condition characterized by severe regression after a few years of normal development)

So What Is Autism?

All children are different. Some children are good in math but, for some, math is quite challenging; some children are good in art, and some find art quite challenging; some children are good in music, and some couldn't carry a tune if their lives depended on it; and so on. Some children are good in language, and some find language quite challenging; some like to socialize, and some find socializing quite challenging.

Autism is a developmental disorder that is characterized by deficits in language and social interaction, and by restricted, repetitive and stereotypical patterns of behaviour, interests, and activities. Children with "autism" don't behave the way they do because they have autism; they have been given that diagnostic label because they

[3] Some people refer to all of the Pervasive Developmental Disorders as Autism Spectrum Disorders.

have a neurological condition that results in language/communication and social relating deficits (and sometimes other problems as well), and these deficits tend to isolate a person (hence the term "autism").

Asperger's Disorder is somewhat similar to Autism, but without such a clear-cut language deficit. As a result, most children with Asperger's Disorder are not given that diagnostic label until they enter school. PDD - NOS (Pervasive Developmental Disorder - Not Otherwise Specified) shares some of the same characteristics as Autism and Asperger's Disorder, but doesn't quite meet the criteria for either of them.

Myths About Autism

It is a myth that autism is caused by poor parenting. In fact, Autism is due to a neurological dysfunction of unknown origin(s). It is not due to an inadequacy of parenting.

It is a myth that autism is rare. In fact, the Autism Spectrum Disorders are more common in children than cancer, diabetes and Down Syndrome. Prevalence is estimated to be about 1 in 150 (and in some locations, 1 in 75).

It is a myth that children with autism live in a world of their own that is no worse than anyone else's world. In fact, people need people, and this is no less true of children with autism. Except for the frustration that their efforts brings them, they do want to be able to communicate and they do want to be able to relate socially – as demonstrated by what happens when they are taught these skills.

It is a myth that children with autism aren't interested in developing friendships. In fact, while it is true that, for children with autism, friendship may not be the highest priority – survival (in a world of social and communicative isolation and sensory confusion) may take precedence – but they will certainly want to have friends at some stage in their development, so it is going to be important that they learn how to develop friendships.

It is a myth that children with autism can be expected to be either mentally challenged or exceptionally bright. In fact, Autism is fairly independent of general intelligence; some individuals with autism are intellectually gifted and some are intellectually challenged.

However, since autism is defined by a delay in communication skills and in social/emotional relationship skills, children with autism will be delayed in these areas of development, and they may score low on tests of general intelligence for those reasons, regardless of their intellectual capacity or potential.

It is a myth that children with autism do not make progress, or that they do not make progress beyond any particular age. In fact, everyone can learn, to a greater or lesser degree, and the ability to learn lasts forever. Although the bulk of our learning does tend to take place while we are young, learning is something that goes on throughout one's life.

It is a myth that children with autism are just trying to be difficult – you should be so lucky!

But This One is Not a Myth

About thirty percent of individuals with autism have difficulty modulating their sensory and motor systems. They may be:

Over-sensitive or under-sensitive to visual stimulation

Over-sensitive or under-sensitive to auditory stimulation

Over-sensitive or under-sensitive to olfactory stimulation

Over-sensitive or under-sensitive to taste stimulation

Over-sensitive or under-sensitive to tactile stimulation

They may also have:

difficulty starting, continuing, stopping, combining, and/or switching movements

and some children with autism have mental and emotional processing issues, as shown by differences in:

perception

attention

consciousness (and confusion)

motivation

emotional regulation – Gillingham (2000) has even suggested that this is the main problem in autism

These sensory, sensorimotor and internal processing variables can make life difficult for the child, and the child's expression of that difficulty may show up as insistence on sameness, repetitive self-stimulatory behaviours ("stimming"), anxiety, depression, anger, or even a complete inability to function (i.e., system shutdown). Parents are advised to try to accommodate to these sensory and internal processing problems by modifying the environment to the extent that it is feasible, and try to enlist the help of an Occupational Therapist (an OT). Then, go ahead and help your child to learn as best he or she can.

You might like to have a look at one or more of the following references,[4] since they provide many suggestions for both accommodating to and treating sensory, sensorimotor and related issues:

The Sensory-Sensitive Child by Smith and Gouze (2004)

The Out-of-Sync Child by Kranowitz (1998)

The Out-of-Sync Child Has Fun by Kranowitz (2003)

Building Bridges through Sensory Integration by Yack, Sutton and Aquilla (1998)

Autism and the Role of Education in Its Treatment

Why do children with ASD have the problems that they do? Nobody knows, although there is lots of speculation. The term "Autism" is descriptive rather than explanatory. However, to the extent that language and/or social interaction aren't learned automatically, they have to be taught (if you want them to be learned).

You should know that there are many different approaches to treating children with autism (see Evidence-Based Practices for Children and Adolescents with Autism Spectrum Disorders, 2003, available from Children's Mental Health Ontario, 416-921-2109, www.cmho.org). However, if learning occurs as a result of any of these different approaches, it will occur in keeping with "the laws of learning" – the conditions under which learning works – as established by research carried out mainly by psychologists during the past century or so.

There are several lines of research into learning, but the three kinds of learning that have been most fully researched are:

---

[4] Although you should be aware that Sensory Integration Training has relatively little research support at present.

Classical conditioning (which was extensively studied by Pavlov and his colleagues and students)
Operant conditioning (which was extensively studied by Skinner and his colleagues and students)
"Social Learning Theory" (which was extensively studied by Walters and Bandura and their colleagues and students)

Classical (or Pavlovian) Conditioning

In classical conditioning, a stimulus becomes able to elicit a particular response by virtue of having been paired with a stimulus that already elicits that response. For example: Suppose your child likes milk. The child will develop a liking for the person who provides the milk, simply by virtue of that person having been paired with the milk (unless, of course, that person is also associated with experiences that the child finds unpleasant). This kind of learning through association – which occurs within the context of "pairing" – has a very important part to play in your child's development.

Operant Conditioning

If some particular behaviour is followed immediately and consistently by a particular consequence, the child will learn to associate that particular consequence with that particular behaviour.

If a behavioural response to some particular antecedent event (or cue) is followed immediately and consistently by a particular consequence, the child will learn to associate that particular consequence with that behavioural response to that antecedent.

Certain consequences – most often, consequences that the child experiences as rewarding – result in the child learning to give a particular response to a particular antecedent. We call those kinds of consequences "reinforcers," because they "reinforce" or strengthen the probability that the child will give that particular response to that particular antecedent. Let me say it again: "If the child learns to give a particular response to a particular antecedent, it is usually safe to assume that, from the point of view, that consequence was desirable or rewarding," [5]

---

[5] Punishment, in contrast to reinforcement, is defined as "a consequence that decreases the likelihood of a child exhibiting the particular behaviour that it follows." As a general rule, consequences that the child finds aversive are likely to

- or to put it another way (although also from a cognitive perspective): if, from the child's point of view, that consequence is desirable or rewarding, the child learns to give that response to that antecedent in the future.[6] That is, the student learns to behave in a particular way because those behaviours are followed by certain kinds of (reinforcing) consequences. This is known as operant conditioning – the child's learning of the behavioural response is conditional upon its having being followed immediately by a consequence which we presume is, from the child's point of view, desirable or rewarding.[7] Learning through reinforcement has a very important part to play in your child's development.

Social Learning Theory

The work of Bandura and Walters and their students on Social Learning Theory (beginning with Social Learning and Personality Development, 1963) included study of the role of modelling in

---

function as punishers. However, this is not always the case, and the only sure way to determine what consequences will function as punishment for the child is to present the consequence after the behaviour and see whether it decreases the likelihood of the child exhibiting that particular behaviour – remember, that is how punishment is defined. You should know, however, that there are lots of problems with the whole idea of punishment, and it is almost never advocated by anyone knowledgeable about teaching children to behave the way we would want them to behave.

[6] Although, technically speaking, whether or not the consequence was perceived by the child as rewarding is immaterial; all that matters is that the probability of the child exhibiting that behaviour in response to that particular antecedent stimulus increases as a result of having been followed by that particular consequence.

[7] As a general rule, consequences that the child finds rewarding are likely to be good reinforcers; but this is not always the case, and the only sure way to determine what will be reinforcing for the child is to present the consequence after the behaviour and see whether the behaviour is strengthened – remember, that is how reinforcement is defined. Nevertheless, for all practical purposes, you should reward any behaviour that you want the child to learn to do.

Experience with this kind of learning has shown that you really don't have to worry about always having to reward your child for everything that he/she does because, once the behaviour has been learned, you can and must gradually cut back on how often you specifically reward the child for each of those behaviours. In addition, most of the behaviours that you will be teaching will eventually generate their own rewards – in fact, just being able to do something new can be rewarding in itself, as the child will eventually discover for him- or herself.

learning, including video modelling, as a way of teaching social behaviours. The learning principle involved is learning through observation. Learning through observation has a very important part to play in your child's development.

ABA and the Science of Teaching Children with Autism

For children with autism, Applied Behaviour Analysis (ABA) may be thought of as remedial education for the language/ communication and social relating deficits, and treatment for the behavioural rigidities, which define autism. It makes use of each of these kinds of learning. It is one of the few approaches that research – as contrasted with anecdotal reports – has demonstrated to be helpful with this population. However, it is primarily a behavioural approach to learning. Based primarily on operant conditioning, it is concerned with observable behaviours. (Why observable behaviours? Because, if you can't see the result of your teaching – in fact, if you can't measure it – it is hard to tell, with any precision, just what is being learned).

However, while ABA relies heavily on "reinforcement" (one of the most important concepts in the teaching of behaviours), it begins with "pairing." (Remember pairing? – from classical conditioning: When things happen at the same time, we learn to associate them with each other). But to understand the role of pairing in an ABA program, it is first necessary to know something about reinforcement and the role pairing plays in reinforcement.

Reinforcement

Reinforcement is a consequence that occurs immediately after some observable behaviour and results in the learning (i.e., the strengthening or "reinforcing") of that particular behaviour. It can be the provision of something desirable, such as a piece of cookie (positive reinforcement) or the removal of something undesirable, such as the removal of some task demand (negative reinforcement). It is much harder to find appropriate negative reinforcers than it is to find appropriate positive reinforcers, so "think positive."

Fortunately, at some point in the learning process, language, social interaction, and social approval/praise can become enjoyable for the child and, therefore, likely to be reinforcing in and of themselves. At that point, the instructor doesn't have to be continually available to keep reinforcing language and social behaviours with arbitrary consequences (such as toys and edibles) in order for the child to continue to engage in them.

Arbitrary aversive consequences (such as spanking and/or yelling at the child) interfere with the learning of behaviours that you will want to teach (e.g., as a substitute for any undesirable behaviours that you want to get rid of), so don't use them! Instead, think of teaching (mainly through providing reinforcement for) the behaviours that you want to get.[8]

Reinforcement can occur in response to every instance of a behaviour (a continuous reinforcement schedule) or less frequently (an intermittent reinforcement schedule). Moving from a continuous reinforcement schedule to an intermittent one is known as "thinning the reinforcement schedule." Behaviour that is maintained through intermittent reinforcement is less susceptible to extinction (i.e., being forgotten/dying out when the reinforcement stops coming regularly) than behaviour that has received only continuous reinforcement. Therefore, "thin the reinforcement schedule" – gradually move from reinforcing every instance of a behaviour to only reinforcing it occasionally – as opportunity permits (but neither so quickly nor so much that the behaviour you are trying to teach is no longer worth the effort to the child).

Reinforcement can be either

(1) innate/built in/hardwired (which we refer to as primary reinforcement) or

(2) learned (which we refer to as secondary reinforcement).

Examples of primary reinforcement include:

- Food – pieces of cookie, chips, etc.
- Drink – water, pop, juice, etc.
- For some children, sensory stimulation – cuddles, tickles, bouncing, swinging, music, etc.

---

[8] Because children tend to engage in desirable behaviours much more frequently than they engage in ubdesirable behaviours, parents, for the sake of efficiency, tend to conserve their energy by focusing mainly on the undesirable behaviours. If that is what you are doing and it isn't working for you, as it probably isn't, try focusing on those behaviours that you wish to encourage rather than those that you wish to have go away. As the old saying goes, "Catch them being good."

- For some children, a decrease in sensory stimulation (because some children with autism, who don't have very good sensory filters, already feel overstimulated).

Secondary reinforcers are learned reinforcers. They come to have their reinforcement value through being paired with something that is already reinforcing (either primary reinforcement or previously-learned secondary reinforcement). The learning principle involved in pairing is learning through association – also known as classical (or Pavlovian) conditioning.

Any reinforcement that has to be learned is, by definition, Secondary Reinforcement. Examples might (or might not, in your child's case) include:

- approval
- social interaction (or even your very presence)
- toy play (other than the lining up of objects, spinning wheels on toy cars, etc. that is so characteristic of children with autism)

If any of these are going to be reinforcers, their reinforcement value may have to be taught (through pairing them with other reinforcers).[9]

Establishing the Reinforcement Value of Social Approval

For most children, social approval is both rewarding and reinforcing, and behaviours followed by social approval are likely to be learned. For many children with autism, however, social approval is a yet-to-be-learned reinforcer. That is, it is not particularly reinforcing until after it has been paired repeatedly with more tangible reinforcers such as food or activities that the child finds rewarding (i.e., activities that are reinforcing for the child). So, begin by pairing yourself and your approval with more tangible reinforcers, until your approval has reinforcement value. Then, continue to pair your approval with other reinforcers once in a while, so that its reinforcement value doesn't fade

[9] Hint: If you take the time to teach a "generalized" secondary reinforcer, e.g., a sound such as a "snap," "tap," or "click," you will find that it can be used very unobtrusively and effectively to mark out for the child those behaviours that you would like him or her to learn. For a fuller discussion of this technique, you might refer to www.tagteach.com

away. Remember, continue to pair your approval with other reinforcers once in a while, so that its reinforcement value doesn't fade away.

At the same time, expose your child to lots of language and fun things that you do together – pair yourself with lots of non-demand "narrative" language[10] and non-demand social interaction – and, of course, reinforce any positive response that you get. But don't talk all of the time. There is also value in pairing yourself with comfortable silence – just quietly being together – if you can learn to use it productively.

To the extent that it is feasible, try not to pair yourself with aversive consequences (i.e., things that the child experiences as unpleasant), such as taking the child from a more rewarding situation to a less rewarding situation, as is likely to occur if you prevent the child's repetitive behaviours (referred to as "stimming") or take him away from playing, etc., unless you are taking him to something that is even more rewarding/reinforcing.

Imagine that the child has three levers he can push:

- escape/avoidance
- repetitive behaviour(s)
- participating with you in enjoyable activities within which learning can occur.

Your job is to arrange conditions so that the child is motivated to push the learning activities lever. He/she will do that if it brings him/her sufficient reward, compared to the effort that it requires of him/her.

---

[10] Also called "declarative" language, in contrast to "imperative" language. Imperative communication uses language forms that are "instrumental" in their objectives – they demand something specific of the child – and they imply that the instructor's point of view is the only one worth considering. Examples of imperative language are:

directives ("Touch the car")

choices ("Would you like the car or the bubbles?")

questions ("What is your name?").

Declarative communication uses language forms that don't make any direct demands on the listener. It tends to involve relative thinking processes which imply that, between two speakers, there can be different views of reality. Examples of declarative language include:

invitations ("Let's play with cars")

statements ("I'm tired of playing with cars!")

self-narratives ("I'm walking over to the table to get a car.)

Don't turn every interaction into one in which demands are being placed on your child – at first, most interactions should be for fun. And, of course, just because many later interactions are formally designed to facilitate learning doesn't mean that they can't also be fun. After all, "Play is a child's work!" and it is within the context of play that most of the work is done to prepare your child for more formal instruction. Play not only provides the main setting in which children learn and practice both language and social skills; it also provides a setting in which you, as instructor, can practice pairing, modelling and reinforcement.[11]

As a general rule, children like to play at those things that either:

(1) bring them enjoyment or

(2) bring them comfort/help them avoid distress.

Most children like to play because of the enjoyment that it brings them. Many children with autism, because of their sensory sensitivities and the stress they experience due to their difficulty communicating and socializing, are more concerned with avoiding distress; and the activities in which they immerse themselves might be called "comfort activities." They are not yet at the stage where they can derive much enjoyment from the kinds of play activities that most children choose to engage in. They actually need help to learn to get enjoyment out of the ordinary kinds of play.

Melinda Smith (Teaching Playskills to Children with Autistic Spectrum Disorder) says that "To have a thorough understanding of play development, you should be familiar with a variety of classifications. These classifications can then serve as general guides to the level of the child's development and need for intervention." We will look at some of these classifications of play next.

Stages of Play: Melinda Smith

Imitative play

Interactive play with adults

---

[11] This is true not only of children with autism, but of children in general; and it is where instruction should begin for many beginning learners, particularly those whose autistic characteristics are part of a larger picture that encompasses significant general developmental challenges.

Independent play

Parallel play with peers

Interactive play with peers

Pretend play

Pretend play with peers

Play in later childhood: Games with rules, sports, video games, "hanging out," roller skating, after school clubs, etc.

Stages of Play: Westby

Westby's Symbolic Play Scale (in Maurice, Green & Luce, Behavioral Intervention…) lists the following stages of play (examples only):

Awareness that objects exist when not seen, e.g., finding toy hidden under scarf

Purposeful exploration of toys

Playful awareness of pretending, e.g., pretending to drink from a cup

Symbolic play with dolls, action figures, etc.

Copying others: representing (re-presenting) daily activities, e.g., playing house, etc.

Copying others: Less frequent activities, e.g., playing doctor/nurse, etc.

Copying others: The wider world, e.g., Fisher-Price toys, dolls as participants in play. Play now has a sequence.

Beginning problem-solving, play involves conceptualization, e.g., child builds an enclosure for animals and thinks his/her way through what to use for a roof.

Fully cooperative play. Plans a sequence of events and helps organize self and others, e.g., pretend store, pretend camping, etc.

Stages of Play: McAlpine

McAlpine lists the following stages of play:

Sensory Stage

- One sensory modality used to explore object
- Several sensory modalities used

Cause and Effect Stage

- Child does one action repeatedly
- Child does more than one action with an object
- Child play is creative; child explores how and why something happens

Doll Play Represents Self and Others

- Child shows curiosity about dolls or figures but doesn't respond to them if they "speak"
- Child responds to doll if it "speaks"
- Child changes voice to make a doll "speak"
- Child changes voice to make a doll "speak," using one doll after another
- Child uses several dolls that "speak" to each other.

Note that this is still parallel play

Stages of Play: Interactive and Cooperative Play

- As a general rule, children learn their early playskills from adults; then they learn to use these same playskills with peers.
- It is desirable, perhaps even necessary, for the child to practice with adults before playing games with other children.
- Early play with peers begins with parallel play and then evolves into interactive and co-operative play.
- Beginning interactive activities might include action songs, crafts, swimming, running in the sprinkler, Playdough, turning summersaults, baking things together, digging in the dirt, etc.
- In later childhood, children move from pretend play to games with rules, e.g., sports, board games, card games, video games, etc.
- And gradually, play becomes more social, e.g., conversing, biking, roller skating, dancing, etc.

Stages of Play: the ABLLS

The Assessment of Basic Language and Learning Skills (the ABLLS) lists the following steps in the beginning development of play:

- Exploring the toys in his/her environment.
- Plays with the toys as intended/designed.
- Plays with toys with an identifiable theme, e.g., dolls, action figures, garage, cooking.
- Talks while playing independently.
- Plays interactively with other children.
- Sociodramatic play.

Stages of Play: Greenspan

Dr. Stanley Greenspan was interested in helping the child establish social/emotional relationships (and sets out to do so within the context of play). He posited six functional developmental levels:

1. Shared attention and attachment
2. Engagement
3. Two way communication
4. Complex two-way communication
5. Shared meanings and symbolic play
6. Emotional thinking

Greenspan proposed to help the child negotiate these six developmental levels through play, starting with activities at the child's "comfort zone," i.e., those activities in which the child currently finds comfort, such as: Lining up blocks, turning lights off and on, spinning things, making noises, deep pressure, etc., etc.[12]

At Levels 1 & 2 (Shared Attention and Engagement):

---

[12] Introductions to Greenspan's Developmental, Individual Differences, Relationship-Based (DIR) model – "Floortime" – can be downloaded from the following websites:

www.coping.org/

www.polyxo.com/floortime/buildingplaypartnerships.html

and from

www.floortime.org

The child still prefers "comfort zone" activities

He/she can pay attention to, tolerate, and/or enjoy brief interactions:

There may be evidence of attachment

The child responds to comfort and attention

The child enjoys sensory-motor play

There is limited receptive language, e.g., the child turns to his or her name occasionally

Interactions are brief and/or inconsistent

At Levels 3 & 4 (Two-way Communication):

There is more sustained engagement: The child seeks attention, comforting; he/she imitates simple gestures

He/she initiates interactions based on needs/wants

He/she enjoys sensory-motor games

Receptive language is more consistently emerging

Gestures are combined with an increasing number of words

There is understanding of basic emotional themes, e,g., approval, alarm, etc.

At Level 5 (Shared Meanings):

The child communicates ideas through words

He/she engages in simple pretend play with adults

And in simple pretend play with children

He/she understands facial expressions

He/she responds to 1 & 2 step commands

There is emerging self concept (e.g., body parts)

There is a developing sense of humour

He/she spontaneously greets familiar people

At Level 6 (Emotional Thinking):

The child expresses and identifies own and others feelings

He/she recognizes a relationship between feelings, behaviour and consequences

There is more complex social dramas/play with themes

He/she takes someone else's view

He/she is aware of social norms

He/she is aware of safety, time, the past, etc.

He/she talks in paragraphs

There are multiple sequences of interactions

The Play Project

You can and, I believe, should also purchase the DVD, The P.L.A.Y. Project Workshop Level 1: Play and Language for Autistic Youngsters by Richard Solomon, MD. This DVD contains a complete workshop, including play-based interventions, based on Greenspan's DIR model.[13] It suggests a variety of playtime approaches and activities appropriate for use by parents at each of Greenspan's developmental levels:

Levels 1 & 2 play activities might include

- Gently shaking arms or legs
- Gently squeezing arms, legs, head
- Swinging in a blanket
- Gentle pressure
- Gentle wrestling
- Tickling
- Blowing on skin, hair, face

---

[13] In contrast to most ABA based interventions, The P.L.A.Y. Project (playproject.org) is specifically designed to be a parent training approach, somewhat similar to Gutstein's Relationship Development Intervention (RDI), which will be discussed later in this publication. "It is primarily designed to help parents be their child's best play partner." (Solomon, R. (2008). Play-based Intervention for Very Young Children with Autism: The P.L.A.Y. Project. In C.E. Schaefer, S. Kelly-Zion, J. McCormick, and A. Ohnogi (Eds). Play Therapy for Very Young Children. Lanham, MD: The Scarecrow Press).

- Opening and closing a door while playing peek-a-boo from the other side
- Water play of all kinds
- Turning the lights off and on
- A "feeling box" (a shoe box filled with beans, or marbles, or Brillo pads, etc.)
- Spinning the child on a swing or swivel chair
- Building blocks up and knocking them down, with accompanying commentary
- Dropping things, with accompanying "Boom"
- Flipping pages of a book

Levels 3 & 4 play activities might include

- All of the Levels 1 & 2 activities
- Chase: "I'm going to get you"
- Get the bubbles, balloon, etc.
- Rolling a ball back and forth
- Very simple pretend play, such as phone to ear, feeding the dolly, cars crash and make a crashing sound
- Finger painting
- Puzzles
- Play with farm animals, dump trucks, trains
- Being silly
- Song games such as "Wheels on the bus," "Eensy weensy spider," "Old MacDonald"
- Building forts from cardboard boxes, tents from blankets over chairs, etc.
- Ready-set-go games
- Making choices about what they want to play
- Getting in the way games ("It's stuck. Can you open it?")
- Remember to follow the child's lead.

Levels 5 & 6 play activities might include

- Pretend: dress up, doll (or action figure) tea party, dinosaurs chasing each other
- Hide and seek
- Reading to the child (and vice versa) – probably mainly looking at the pictures and talking about what is happening in the story line
- Drawing faces
- Sequencing cards, objects, etc.
- Tic-tac-toe
- Musical chairs
- Tag
- Treasure hunts
- Simon says
- Board games: Snakes and ladders
- Card games: Fish
- Jokes
- I spy
- More complex pretend games

Contrasting Floortime and behavioural approaches, Greenspan suggested the following differences:

Play-Based	**Behavioural**
! Strategic & Flexible!	More prescribed
! More naturalistic!	More controlled
! Child initiated!	Program oriented
! Follows child's lead!	Program goals dominant
! Affect emphasized!	Behaviour emphasized
! Documentation varies!	Documentation intensive

In my opinion, it is unfortunate that Greenspan, in his writings, tended to provide a lot of misinformation about ABA, as it is (or should be) currently practiced. It was not his area of expertise – Greenspan was, after all, psychodynamically-oriented rather than behaviourally-oriented – so remember that what he has said about ABA has to be "taken with a grain of salt." The above-listed differences, however, do exist; and I believe that they are the reason that behavioural programs based on the principles of ABA have been demonstrated to be effective with this population.

Nevertheless, Floortime has many useful ideas – such as the idea of getting "down on the floor" and playing with your child, particularly in the beginning (as a precursor to more formal ABA-based instruction) – in spite of the fact that, *to date, research suggests that relationship-based programs don't accomplish as much as more structured teaching/learning activities;* and personally, I much prefer to use ABA as the main conceptual model for any formal teaching.[14]

In addition to promoting his model of treatment (Floortime), Greenspan was one of the driving forces behind the Interdisciplinary Council on Developmental and Learning Disorders. If you wish, you may go to www.icdl.com and download their Clinical Practice Guidelines. This runs to about 1000 pages and covers a wide range of autism-related topics. Much of this information you are not likely to find assembled into an easy-to-reference package anywhere else and, while I am not very enthusiastic about several of the approaches presented in these "Guidelines," all of them do contain some useful ideas.

A Few Playskills References

"Giggle Time," and "Playing, Laughing and Learning with Children on the Autism Spectrum" and Floortime are all good resources for teaching a beginning learner how to begin to relate

---

[14] It has been pointed out to me that DIR/Floortime does not claim to be a "formal teaching method" (Mike Fields, Oct 2006). However, it seems to me that Floortime does claim to be a way of promoting the child's development, and learning does seem to be the mechanism through which such "promoting" occurs. A distinction can be made between cognitive learning and emotional learning, but I see no reason to believe that either of these types of learning is exclusive to either Floortime or ABA. Both Floortime and ABA can be used to promote the child's cognitive development and both can be used to promote the child's emotional development.

socially; and it looks to me as if "Playing, Laughing and Learning..." is a bit of a cross between Floortime and a more formal ABA kind of teaching, so it ought to be a good resource. "More Than Words" and "The Autistic Spectrum Parents' Daily Helper" are good next-step resources in parent-and-child-with-autism interaction. "Teaching Playskills to Children with Autistic Spectrum Disorder" by Melinda Smith has lots of good suggestions for teaching playskills. "Games Babies Play" by Vicki Lansky has lots of good ideas for beginning learners. Several of the books listed in the next few pages (See A Few Other Books and Resources That You May Want to Examine) also contain a myriad of suggestions for games and activities of potential interest to children, and you can also find a ton of ideas at: www.melindasmith.home.mindspring.com

Finally, for a set of notes regarding one family's experience in teaching playskills, you might have a look at:

www.members.tripod.com/~RSaffran/play.html

Prelude to Formal Instruction: Beginning Social Relationships

Once they have counted a newborn's fingers and toes, the next thing that parents look for is some kind of emotional response. They want their child to provide them with what is called "emotional reciprocity," a positive response to their positive response to the child. They want to see face-to-face gazing – as an indication that the child has noticed their attempts to relate and communicate, as well as to intensify everyone's joy and excitement and to sooth the child's distress.

Giggle Time – Establishing the Social Connection

The book, Giggle Time, like Greenspan's approach (Floortime), is about the process of developing these conjoint action routines (communication) between adult and child. "The adult looks for behaviors in the child that might be interpreted as communicative. He or she then shapes those behaviors by responding in an interesting way." (We will tell you more about shaping later). The parent, for example, reinforces a sideways glance, a hesitation, a vocalization so the child will do it again, and that same interaction continues for some minutes. Follow the child's lead until he/she gives you something to which you can respond. Then try to turn it into a simple, silly game/routine.

Be prepared to offer yourself as a participant in that game for ten minutes or so if the child remains interested in it. Through the adult's consistent response – a tickle, a sudden movement, a sound – to a particular "communicative" behaviour by the child, the child learns (1) that he/she can predictably influence his/her environment and (2) that it can be enjoyable to do so. When all else fails, you can always fall back on just imitating the child's own sounds and actions.

Beginning Social Relationships: Joint Attention

As the child begins to initiate these enjoyable reciprocal interactions through drawing to the adult's attention what he/she is interested in at the moment, he/she demonstrates what is known as "joint attention," one of the hallmarks of social development.[15] Joint attention typically happens long before the development of language.

Beginning Social Relationships: Referencing

For success in life, the child needs to learn, as a typical next step in the process of socialization, to reference other people – their facial expressions and gestures – as a guide to his/her own behaviour. He/she will learn to do so if good things happen when he/she does this kind of referencing (similar to what happens when you are attempting to establishing "instructional control," the first step in formal instruction – to be discussed later).

The Importance of Nonverbal Communication

Note that referencing, like joint attention, is nonverbal since, at the beginning stages of the child's development, communication is mainly nonverbal. Note also that, at later stages, communication continues to be mainly nonverbal. In everyday interaction, nonverbal communication carries about 55% of the information being conveyed. Nonverbal communication is an essential part of successful social interaction.

---

[15] Of course, for joint attention to flourish, it is necessary for the child's efforts to elicit a positive response. You cannot ignore your child's attempts to communicate if you want your child to learn to talk; and you would not believe the number of times that I have seen parents ignoring their child's communication attempts while, at the same time, complaining about the fact that their child doesn't talk!

Playing With Your Child

Remember that play is, first of all, for fun, with the learning of specific things being part of the fun! Both narrate what is happening, particularly for you, (but not too intrusively) and participate in it. One of the biggest mistakes parents make is turning play into work by asking a lot of questions!

If you find that your child gets too excited with a particular activity or toy, take a break and then come back with something else. Never give up on your efforts to engage your child.

Now, it may seem like I am overemphasizing play, but I don't believe that I am. There is a place for work, just as there is a place for play. Nevertheless, there is a lot wrong with ABA as it is practiced by many of the service providers that I know, most of which can be easily corrected by placing a greater emphasis on play, as recommended by Robert Schramm in Educate Toward Recovery (2006), the book which I tend to think of as the "ABA Bible":

> "Many prior therapy procedures were designed around teaching in the intensive trial teaching (ITT) environment. Table teaching was rote and repetitive. Because of the inflexible and often counterproductive procedures used in ABA during that time, children were not encouraged to seek or desire social interaction nor did the method foster interaction or experience sharing. ... Consequently, many children were inept when it came to forming relationships with others.[16] Although attempts were made to help socialise these children, they were often incapable of adapting to new situations or people and were unable to form meaningful or lasting friendships." (p. 264).

> "In the best ABA/VB Programs approximately 75% of every interaction you have with your child should be reserved for the process of pairing yourself with fun activities and known reinforcement. Pairing activities should be led by your child's motivation and should include only non-verbal and

---

[16] And remember that autism is defined as much by deficits in social interaction as by deficits in communication. That social interaction deficit is what is usually left even after the child has mastered the nuts-and-bolts of communication as represented by, for example, completion of most of the items on the ABLLS-R (which will be discussed later).

declarative language. ***Declarative language*** is language that asks for nothing of your child. It only serves to share your thoughts and feelings. This is important language for your child to learn and should be modeled to your child throughout your interactions." (p. 46).[17]

"The problem with pairing as a concept in ABA/VB is that it is not well defined. ***Pairing is a process of playing with your child.*** [Bold italics added for emphasis. RMR] Thus, making his daily experience more enjoyable when he is with you than when he is without you. Good pairing does not include the use of S^Ds (instructions). In fact, it only took about one page of this book to explain how best to pair with your child. If you think about it, only one page of what you have read so far discusses what you should be doing with 75% of the time you are with your child. The remainder of this book discusses in extreme detail what you should be doing during the 25% of the time you are not engaged in pairing procedures." (p. 267).

"To pair yourself with reinforcement, follow your child's interests and offer him access to play with anything he is interested in as long as you are allowed to play along with him. Make his playtime more fun because *you* are a part of it." (p. 46).

"It is during the 75% of time spent pairing with a child, that you are a purposely not eliciting, prompting, or reinforcing responses. It is only during this pairing time that the child is allowed to make the necessary choices to explore the joy of others and spontaneously share of feelings of his own.[18] Similar to the beliefs of RDI, TM I feel that the way to teach social experience sharing and a desire for social

---

[17] ***Imperative language***, in contrast, "is any form of language that expects something in return." (p.48). "You should only be using imperative language during the 25% of your interaction with your child in which you are not engaged in pairing." (p. 48).

[18] Although, at another point, Schramm does say: "Start by pairing with your child. This means getting involved in some fun reinforcing activity in which he wants your participation. In the beginning, avoid directions or S^Ds. Your goal is strictly to get him laughing and enjoying being with you. ... Begin to incorporate a few small and easy S^Ds into the play. Make them things that your child is most likely to do without thinking. Many times, skills that you know your child has recently mastered work well here. Be sure to reward those responses appropriately with more and better play." (p.194).

relationships is in large part through the 75% of teaching time that we are simply pairing with a child." (p. 268).

Regarding the relationship between pairing and teaching, Mary Barbera (The Verbal Behavior Approach, 2007) notes that, once you determine what your child already likes, the next step is to pair yourself and the area that will become the child's work area with those items and/or activities, until both become secondary reinforcers (i.e., until both are perceived by the child as desirable). "When work begins – and it should begin once the child is happily approaching the work area – it's important that the child does not really know that he is working." (2007, p.67). The child should not be able to notice the transition from nothing-but-pairing to the situation in which something is being asked of him/her. Demands should be increased very gradually and should never make up more than a small part of the instructional program – as Schramm says, even when an instructional program is well established, 75% of your interactions with your child should still consist of pairing yourself with reinforcement, and instruction (which so often places specific demands on the child, i.e., for correct answers) should make up no more than 25% of your interactions with him or her.[19] He reports that, when one of his instructors and/or parents strays very far from this 75:25 ratio, teaching tends to become more of a negative experience for the child than a positive one, more a case of "If you work hard for me, I will give you a break from instruction" rather than something that the child can't wait to seek out; and this has been my experience as well.[20]

---

[19] Suppose that you will be working with a child for two hours. Do not spend the first hour and a half pairing yourself with reinforcement and the final half hour providing instruction. These activities are to be interlaced – little bits of instruction inserted into your playtime so that, as Barbera says, "the child does not really know that he is working." Of course, all children are different, and the occasional child will let you know in no uncertain terms that he/she wants to work. I know of more than one child that behaves like a sponge – they just want to learn everything that you can teach them – but that is more the exception than the rule.

[20] And note that the child does not have to be high functioning to be eager to participate in ABA-based instruction. I have seen a child who could do little more than correctly place the remaining piece of a simple six piece puzzle (when the other five pieces had already been put in place) dragging her mother into the work area because she couldn't wait to get started on her morning's instruction! Obviously, she was getting a lot of satisfaction from her efforts (and probably partly from the achievement itself).

Playdates and Playgroups

When it is time to introduce your child to play with other children, start small and work your way up, e.g., one other child to start with. Before introducing playdates/playgroups, begin by teaching toleration for proximity to other children – mainly through gradual exposure.

Invite a friend or potential friend over – girls who are slightly older than your child often make good playdate peers. Provide activities geared to their level of development, e.g., parallel play, interactive play or co-operative play, with lots of reinforcement for all participants. You will find that you need to walk a fine line between providing enough structure and allowing the children enough freedom to learn to play together. This can be tricky, since typical children are often loud, active, etc., which can over-stimulate a child who has sensory modulation issues; and he/she can seek refuge in repetitive behaviours (i.e., "stimming"). If that happens, you may have tried to move a bit too fast. Just back things off a little, and move up on it again a bit more slowly.

Teach the other children – through instruction and reinforcement – to support your child's learning. Provide lots of reinforcement for all present, e.g., pizza, cookies, pop. Remember, other children become reinforcing through being paired with reinforcement. If they can be the ones to provide the reinforcement, so much the better.

More Precursors to ABA: What to do even before you try to get a formal instructional program started

First of all, it is recommended that you apply for assistance from those agencies providing services for children with autism. Join the local chapter of the Autism Society – in Ontario, AutismOntario – or FEAT and get to know other parents. Many of them have the experience that you need, and they can be a tremendous help to you. There are some excellent resources available from AutismOntario:

Children Diagnosed with Autism: What to Expect and Where to Get Help.

Navigating the Special Education System in Ontario: A Handbook for Parents of Children with Autism Spectrum Disorders.

See www.autismsociety.on.ca or telephone 416 246-9592 for more information (and to locate an AutismOntario chapter near you, if you happen to live in Ontario).

A Few Autism "Lists" that You Might Wish to Join

The Autism list – to subscribe, go to http://lists.apana.org/cgi-bin/mailman/listinfo/autism

The Me-List – send a message to listserv@listserv.iupui.edu and in the message section put: subscribe me-list

The DTT-NET list – go to groups.yahoo.com and <Search> for DTT-NET and subscribe to it

The Verbal Behavior list – go to groups.yahoo.com and <Search> for VerbalBehavior and subscribe to it.

A Few Other Books and Resources That You May Want to Examine as Time Permits

Let Me Hear Your Voice: A Family's Triumph Over Autism by Catherine Maurice (1993) – for inspiration

The Verbal Behavior Approach: How to Teach Children with Autism and Related Disorders by Mary Lynch Barbera (2007) – a goldmine of ABA experience in a relatively small and easy to read book. An excellent book for parents and therapists alike, and a very good place to start.

Educate Toward Recovery: A Teaching Manual for the Verbal Behavior Approach to ABA by Robert Schramm (2006) – If I were only able to recommend one book, this might be it, particularly for its chapters on instructional control, teaching a child who insists on being in control, and the relationship between ABA and RDI. In my opinion, this book should be required reading for everyone working with children with autism, including their parents!

Facing Autism by Lynn Hamilton (2000)

Giggle Time: Establishing the Social Connection by Susan Aud Sonders (2003)

The Autistic Spectrum *Parents' Daily Helper*: A Workbook for You and Your Child by Abrams and Henriques (2004)

More Than Words by Fern Sussman (1999)

Teaching Language to Children with Autism or Other Developmental Disabilities by Sundberg & Partington (1998), the ABLLS-R by Partington (2006)

VB-MAPP: Verbal Behavior Milestones Assessment and Placement Program by Mark Sundberg (2008)

A Work in Progress by Leaf & McEachin (1999)

From Goals to Data and Back Again: Adding Backbone to Developmental Intervention for Children with Autism by Lehman and Klaw (2003/2006)

Relationship Development Intervention with Young Children by Gutstein & Sheely (2002) – Relationship Development Intervention is often referred to by its acronym, RDI.

Relationship Development Intervention with Children, Adolescents and Adults by Gutstein & Sheely (2002)

The RDI Book by Steven Gutstein (2009) – This is another book that should be in every parent's and therapist's library.

Help Us Learn by Kathy Lear (2004) – This is about setting up an ABA program.

Behavioral Intervention for Young Children with Autism by Catherine Maurice (editor) with Green & Luce (1996)

Making a Difference by Maurice, Green & Foxx, Editors (2001), especially for its chapter by Bridget Taylor on "Teaching Peer Social Skills to Children with Autism"

Teaching Individuals with Developmental Delays by Ivar Lovaas (2003)

The Sensory-Sensitive Child: Practical Solutions for Out of Bounds Behavior by Smith and Gouze (2004)

Building Bridges Through Sensory Integration by Yack, Sutton and Aquilla (1998)

Solve Your Child's Sleep Problems by Richard Ferber (1985)

Playing, Laughing and Learning with Children on the Autism Spectrum by Julia Moor (2002)

Teaching Playskills to Children with Autistic Spectrum Disorder: A Practical Guide by Melinda Smith (2001)

You're Going to Love This Kid! by Kluth (2003) – This excellent book is about "Teaching Students with Autism in the Inclusive Classroom," and you should ensure that your child's teacher has access to a copy of it.

Inside Out: What Makes a Person with Social-Cognitive Deficits Tick? by Michelle Winner (2000)

Thinking About You Thinking About Me by Michelle Winner (2002)

Reaching Out, Joining In: Teaching Social Skills to Young Children with Autism by Weiss & Harris (2001)

Navigating the Social World by Jeanette McAfee (2002)

Social Skills Solutions: A Hands On Manual for Teaching Social Skills to Children with Autism by Kelly McKinnon and Janis Krempa (2002)

Conversations: A Framework for Language Interventions by Barbara Hoskins (1996)

Functional Behavioral Assessment for People with Autism: Making Sense of Seemingly Senseless Behavior by Beth Glasberg (2006)

What You Need to Know about Motivation and Teaching Games by Steven Ward (2008)

Motivate to Communicate: 300 Games and Activities for Your Child with Autism by Griffin & Sandler (2010) – this book also lists lots of useful websites.

Early Intervention Games by Barbara Sher (2009) – organized by area such as Social Gross Motor Games, Social Fine Motor Games, Water Games

101 Games and Activities with Autism, Asperger's, and Sensory Processing Disorders by Tara Delaney (2009) – this is also organized by area.

Make-Believe Games and Activities for Imaginative Play by Singer & Singer (2001)

Attention Games by Barbara Sher (2006) – "101 Fun, Easy Games That Help Kids Learn to Focus."

Yoga for Children with Autism Spectrum Disorders by Betts & Betts (2006) – I would get this one, since it has many suggestions specific to our population.

YogaKids by Marsha Wenig (2003) – this one beautifully illustrates the poses. Many photos.

A Word of Caution Regarding Recommended Resources

There are, of course, many more excellent books which have not been included in the above list, mainly due to my own inability to keep all of them in mind as I write this brief introduction. I do wish that I could include all of them here, or even that I could keep up with the burgeoning literature in this field!

Remember that the opinions and suggestions offered by the authors of these various books and other resources are no more than that, their opinions and suggestions – and that is what has been called "a college education in a nutshell," the knowledge that you cannot accept something as "truth" just because it's author has managed to get it published. All of this information has to be considered within the context of everything else that you know about your child. I sincerely hope that the information that you are being given in this paper is accurate and that the suggestions are helpful, but you should be aware that this field is changing so fast that much of what you hear today may very well be outdated by next year, if not by next month. As Perry and Condillac observe regarding many of the approaches they reviewed in Evidence-Based Practices for Children and Adolescents with Autism Spectrum Disorders, "If they are used as intervention, they should be monitored and their effects on specific goals empirically assessed, they should be discontinued if there is no evidence of effectiveness, and they should be integrated with other (proven) interventions."

Beginning Formal Instruction

The first step in formal instruction, after beginning to engage your child in mutually-enjoyable activities, is to teach him/her to look to you for instructions (also known as "establishing instructional control." [21] It is similar, but not identical, to what Gutstein – more about him later – calls "establishing a Master-Apprentice relationship"). Typically, this is a smooth extension of the above-mentioned play activities, as the child begins to develop memories of the fun he/she had in things that you did together in the past.

To get your child to look to you for instructions, you have to give instructions, see that the child follows them, and reinforce the (following-of-instructions) behaviour. But you can't teach this directly, since the instructions that you give always have to be specific: Any following-of-instructions that the child learns has to be a generalization he/she makes from many specific teaching/learning trials. That is, you want your child to learn to do what you ask him/her to do and, to do this, he/she has to:

(1) do what you ask him/her to do (when you ask him/her to do it), and

(2) have his/her doing-what-he/she-is-asked-to-do behaviour reinforced for doing so.

That will work best if you never give instructions that you aren't willing to enforce[22] and reinforce. Don't teach your child that he/she doesn't have to do what you ask him/her to do (e.g., by allowing him/her to avoid doing what he/she is asked to do).

Principles of Remedial Education

Now, to put ABA into perspective, here are the principles that govern remedial education:

Determine what the child already knows.

Break the material to be learned into relatively small steps.

Starting where the child is, teach the next steps in each part of the curriculum.

Measure the change.

---

[21] Schramm has an excellent discussion of instructional control in his book, Educate Toward Recovery.

[22] Gross motor behaviours can be physically prompted, but speech cannot. So, since you can't force a child to speak, don't demand it of him/her until he/she has demonstrated a willingness to attempt what you ask of him/her.

Modify your procedures and teaching targets as necessary to ensure continuing progress.

Principles of Applied Behaviour Analysis or How To Teach a Child With Autism

And here are the principles that govern ABA:

Determine what the child already knows.

Break the material to be learned into relatively small steps.

Starting where the child is, teach the next steps in each part of the curriculum.

Measure the change.

Modify your procedures and teaching targets as necessary to ensure continuing progress.

You may notice that they look remarkably similar. ☺

ABA and the Teaching of Observable Behaviours: A Brief Review

Applied Behaviour Analysis (ABA) is a behavioural approach to learning; it is concerned with observable behaviours. (Why observable behaviours? Because, if you can't see it – in fact, if you can't measure it – it is hard to tell whether or not it is being learned).[23] ABA makes a lot of use of Operant principles, in which "learning is as easy as A-B-C" (Antecedent, Behaviour, Consequence).

- **A**ntecedent Conditions (also called the Discriminative Stimulus or S^D) – something that happens just before (and serves as a

---

[23] From Goals to Data and Back Again (Lehman and Klaw, 2003/2006) provides an excellent discussion of how to write measurable behavioral objectives (See p. 44 and following). In general, however, you can expect that a well written objective will "be specific about the variables that surround the desired outcome." For example, the written objective should contain the specific behaviour that you wish to see, the direction of movement (i.e., is it an increase or a decrease in the frequency or the duration or range of some behaviour), the where, when, and with whom you wish that specific behaviour to occur, the level of (prompt) support the child is expect to need in order to demonstrate that behavior, the date by which you expect that objective to be reached, and the type of measurement that you will be using to determine success (e.g., a tally of occurrences, percentage, rating on a qualitative scale).

cue for) the behaviour that you want the child to learn to do as a response to that cue/those antecedent conditions.

- **B**ehaviour – something that the child does in response to that cue/those antecedent conditions.
- **C**onsequences – which increase the likelihood of occurrence of that behaviour when the child is presented with that cue/those antecedent conditions. (Such consequences are said to reinforce, or to be a reinforcer for, the behaviour that they follow).

Teaching Models/Venues: ITT and NET

In this section, I am going to introduce you to some new language, some of which (in my opinion) is pretty close to jargon, so you will have to pay close attention. In most of the older ABA literature, people referred to two common teaching models/venues used in an ABA program: Discrete Trial Teaching (DTT) and Natural Environment Teaching (NET). DTT involved the instructor and student working together at a table, using a series of discrete Antecedent-Behaviour-Consequence "teaching/learning trials," while NET (also known as "incidental teaching," although, personally, I would prefer to reserve the term "incidental teaching" for teaching that is incidental to your stated goals), in contrast, occurred wherever opportunity was presented, i.e., it was conducted in the child's natural environment rather than in a more formal teaching setting, making use of the child's immediate interests and activities in that environment.[24]

Recently, however, some well-known service providers[25] are suggesting that a better distinction would be between Intensive Trial Teaching (ITT) and Natural Environment Teaching (NET), rather than between DTT and NET, at least partly because the teaching trials in NET are also discrete, i.e., each teaching/learning trial has a beginning and an end.

In this new way of looking at things, ITT involves the instructor and student working together at a table, often using as many as 16-25 discrete Antecedent-Behaviour-Consequence "teaching/learning trials" per minute[26] and (in the beginning at least, unless you are teaching

---

[24] NET, as a result, is where parents can really shine!

[25] Holly Kibbe and Cherish Twigg of Establishing Operations, Inc. in a workshop on "Teaching Verbal Behavior in the Natural Environment."

[26] Hence the "intensive" part of ITT.

"requesting," in which case the reinforcement is getting what has been requested) the reinforcement is most often arbitrary (in the sense of being unrelated to what is being learned), i.e., whatever consequence works to strengthen the behaviour being taught, such as a piece of cookie[27] for learning to say "book" when shown a book and asked "What is it?"

Natural Environment Teaching (NET), in contrast, uses the same kind of discrete Antecedent-Behaviour-Consequence "teaching/ learning trials" as ITT but the reinforcement, rather than being arbitrary, is the learner's motivation-of-the-moment. In this way of thinking about NET, "environment" does not refer to location but, rather, to the fact that the reinforcement is natural rather than arbitrary, i.e., the teaching occurs within the "environment" of natural rather than arbitrary reinforcement.[28] NET still makes use of the child's interests and activities of the moment, just as before, and interactions that involve materials and activities which are meaningful to the child, used in a reinforcing manner, continue to be the key to Natural Environment learning, but location is not particularly important.

NET makes use of both stimulus variation and response variation. It requires you to "think on your feet," making use of whatever the child is interested in, or can be interested in, at the moment, to keep him or her engaged in the task of learning. Consequently, it can be a little more challenging for the instructor, but it is more fun than only working at a table; and we do like to keep things fun for both the instructor and the child. In addition, however, there is some research that suggests that "Naturalistic Language Teaching Procedures for Children at Risk for Language Delays" – incidental teaching, modeling, milieu language teaching, etc. – can be even more effective than more structure approaches in facilitating the generalization of children's acquired language skills (Peterson, The Behavior Analyst Today, Vol. No. 5, Issue No. 4, 2004), and that is an extremely

---

[27] Although if you do it right, you should be able to make use of a lot of social reinforcement by the time that you get to implementing ITT.

[28] This is my understanding of what is currently being taught by Holly Kibbe and Cherish Twigg (www.establishingoperationsinc.com) in their workshop on teaching verbal behaviour in the natural environment -- and I hope that is correct, because I really like that way of thinking about it. ☺

important component of making language actually functional for the child.[29]

Establishing Operations Inc. is advocating that the relative amounts of ITT and NET be based on whether the learner is a beginner, an intermediate learner, or an advanced learner – it is recommended that NET be the main teaching model for both beginning and advanced learners (where interpersonal engagement is crucial to program goals) and that ITT be the main teaching model for intermediate learners (where the vast bulk of intermediate language-acquisition goals need to be taught). Of course, it is important to remember that all children are different and that what works well for one child may not work as well for another and that, while a particular approach may work very well at one point in a child's program, it may not work as well later on. One of the main advantages to ABA is that it is data driven, and (in theory, at least) ABA programs are adjusted as needed to ensure the child's continuing progress. As noted in the Behaviour Institute's IBI workshop for parents: "One of the fundamental characteristics of

---

[29] "Intensive Behavioural Intervention: A Workshop for Parents of Young Children with Autism," prepared by Behaviour Institute (Hamilton and Toronto) for the Integrated Services for Children Division of the Ontario Ministry of Community and Social Services when Ontario was developing its IBI program discussed the range of behavioural interventions found within this approach, including Discrete Trail Teaching (DTT, in which an antecedent-response-consequence cycle comprises a trial, or learning opportunity for the child) and Incidental or Natural Environment Teaching (NET, which is teaching that occurs throughout the natural environment, i.e., wherever the child happens to be).

With respect to the latter, it was noted that "Early behavioural approaches to teaching language have tended to see language development in children with autism as a behaviour needing to be taught under tightly controlled environmental conditions, free from distraction. Language instruction tended to be provided in a discrete trial teaching format.... Teaching would be done on a one-to-one basis with seating arrangements and the choice of stimuli being decided by the teacher. There were a number of problems in child outcomes found to be associated with discrete trial teaching of language skills. Gains were slow to occur (Lovaas, 1977). When gains were obtained, they were minimal and associated with failure of the child to generalize spontaneous language outside of the training situation. Finally, teaching language in a discrete trial format was frequently associated with problem behaviours from the child (Koegel, 1996)." (p. 7.2). Thus, language acquisition is now taught through a combination of formats including both DTT – it is now being suggested that this be referred to as ITT – and NET, as appropriate to the task, i.e., some things are best taught in one format and some in another.

applied behaviour analysis is its emphasis on direct and frequent measurement of children's performance as the main basis for making decisions about the child's program." (p. 6.18). I would add that the data not only needs to be collected, it needs to be graphed as well, so that the effectiveness of the teaching can be seen at a glance.

Reinforcement and Shaping

In addition to pairing, the three main issues to be addressed in teaching children are (in my opinion):

Reinforcement

Shaping

Having a very detailed list of the small steps that have to be taught in each area of the child's life

We have already talked a bit about reinforcement, and there are many curricula that will provide you with information about what needs to be taught – we will tell you more about that later – which brings us to shaping. Shaping refers to accepting (for the sake of having a chance to provide the child with reinforcement) any approximation of the behaviour that you wish the child to learn, and then very gradually reinforcing each small incremental step that will eventually lead to the child accurately producing the behaviour that you want him/her to learn.

Shaping is not something new – we do it all the time when teaching beginning learners. For example, we don't expect toddlers to have perfect enunciation before we start providing them with approval for their attempts to talk. We accept what they can produce, and only then do we start to raise our expectations, a little bit at a time. Shaping allows the child to be rewarded for his/her efforts, even if what he/she is able to produce is less than perfect, and that helps to keep him/her motivated to keep trying.[30]

---

[30] In fact, it has recently been suggested that we should always be thinking about shaping whenever there is a response which is less than perfect – that it may be more productive to stop thinking of responses as being either "right" or "wrong," and to begin thinking of them as either "right" or "in-need-of-shaping-into-the-correct-response." Admittedly, this may be more sophisticated than most people are ready to implement at their current stage in learning about ABA, but it is something which could at least be kept in mind for future consideration.

Now for Another Brief Review of ABA Principles

- Start with small teachable steps
- Determine what the child already knows, and starting where the child is, teach the next step or steps in the curriculum, using the ABC model[31]
- Collect data, to keep track of what is being learned
- Use the data as a guide to adjusting your teaching

Variation Among ABA Programs

If a program has the components listed above, then it is an ABA program. However, that still allows for considerable variation among ABA programs. Some (older) programs employ massed trials, i.e., presenting the same antecedent-behaviour-consequence pattern over and over again until it is fully learned, while others prefer to mix and vary their teaching targets. Some (older) programs use "No, no" prompting as a way of alerting the child to his errors, while other programs prefer to strive for "errorless learning," using a lot of what is known as "most-to-least" prompting (I will explain all this in just a few moments). Some (older) programs think of language as being either receptive or expressive, while other programs choose to approach language in terms of its functions: imitating, requesting, labelling, etc. All of these differences within the field of ABA just mean that the treatment of autism is still in its infancy – well, possibly in its adolescence – and that we don't yet know which of these strategies are going to be the most effective way to do ABA.

And, of course, what works best can vary from child to child and moment to moment anyway – in all likelihood, no one approach will work best for all children all of the time. To be most effective, treatment has to be individualized. The question then becomes "Which approach is going to work best for your child right now?"

---

[31] ***Mary Barbera*** (The Verbal Behavior Approach: How to Teach Children with Autism and Related Disorders, 2007) recommends that you limit yourself to about 20 teaching targets at any one time, ***and that each be a small enough step that it can be mastered within a week or two.*** To me, this seems like a very good idea. Again, all children are different, and what is best for one child is not necessarily what is best for another.

Applied Verbal Behaviour and Its Associated Effective Teaching Procedures

Personally, I prefer, as the starting point for any formal ABA program, a particular set of effective teaching procedures which are associated with what has come to be known as Applied Verbal Behaviour (ABA/VB, AVB, or simply VB).[32] Other than the teaching procedures which have come to be associated with it, Applied Verbal Behaviour (or Verbal Behaviour) is nothing more than ABA with an emphasis on teaching language from a functional perspective, i.e., taking into account the various functions of language, such as asking for things, naming things, talking about things, etc. – more about that later.

My two favorite ABA/VB books are:

(1) The Verbal Behavior Approach: How to Teach Children with Autism and Related Disorders by Mary Lynch Barbera (2007) – a goldmine of ABA experience in a relatively small and easy to read book. An excellent book for parents and therapists alike, and a very good place to start.

(2) Educate Toward Recovery: A Teaching Manual for the Verbal Behavior Approach to ABA by Robert Schramm (2006) – If I were only able to recommend one book for someone who really wants to be a good instructor/therapist, this might be it, particularly for its chapters on instructional control, teaching a child who insists on being in control, and the relationship between ABA and RDI.

For more information on Verbal Behaviour, there is a recently developed "wiki" at http://verbalbehavior.pbwiki.com/

Teaching Procedures Associated with ABA/VB

Always try to start and end your interaction with your child on a high note.

---

[32] While these are excellent teaching procedures, you should be aware that they can sometimes work against you. For example, your errorless teaching can teach a child that there is only one right answer to a question, which will sometimes interfere with the development of spontaneous speech; some children sometimes seem to need massed trials in order to learn; and so on. You have to keep track of what is happening – ABA's data collection component – and modify your procedures as necessary to keep your child's program moving along.

Use "Most-to-Least" prompting.

Think "Transfer Trial" – a transfer trial is an opportunity to respond without being prompted. (It is provided after a prompted response)

Mix easy and difficult tasks.

Mix/vary targets and tasks.

Teach to fluency.

Most-to-Least Prompting ("Errorless Learning")

Most-to-Least Prompting, also known as "Errorless Teaching/Learning" [33] refers to the ready use of prompting to ensure the child's success. One way to try to ensure that the child gives the correct response is to model the response that you want to get. Another way to prompt is to guide him/her through the behaviour, providing only as much help as he/she needs to be able to respond correctly.

Prompting is not always needed. However, if it is needed (for the child to be successful on a particular teaching/learning trial), then the time between antecedent and prompt should usually be no more than two or three seconds. And remember that prompts need to be removed from the antecedent-behaviour-consequence sequence (i.e., "faded") as quickly as possible – this is illustrated below – so that the child doesn't become "prompt dependent."

Types of Prompts – Note that some of these prompts ae more intrusive than others, and that the least intrusive effective prompt should be used whenever prompting is needed:

Modelling

Full hand-over-hand prompt

Partial physical prompt

Gestural prompt

Verbal prompt

Visual prompt

Positional prompt

---

[33] Which, you should know, is not necessarily errorless. ☺

etc., etc.

Most-to-Least Prompting: A Verbal Example

Teacher: Showing a cookie or a picture of a cookie, says "What is it?" immediately says, "Cookie." (modeling the correct response, using a verbal prompt)

Child: "Cookie."

Teacher: "Right, it's a cookie. What is it?" (no prompt – a "transfer trial")

Child: "Cookie."

Teacher immediately reinforces the correct response while saying, "That's right, it's a cookie."

Most-to-Least Prompting: A Verbal Example Using Signing

Teacher: Showing a cookie or a picture of a cookie, says "What is it?" immediately signs and says, "Cookie." (modeling the correct response, using the sign and vocalization for cookie)

Child: Sign for "Cookie."

Teacher: "That's right, it's a cookie (signing and saying "cookie"). What is it?" (no prompt – a "transfer trial")

Child: Sign for "Cookie."

Teacher immediately reinforces the correct response while signing and saying "cookie."

Most-to-Least Prompting: An Action Example

Teacher: "Show me brushing."

Child: Child is assisted in brushing, by the teacher taking the child's hand and, using a hand-over-hand prompt, having the child brush his/her hair. Teacher: "That's right, you are brushing."

Teacher: "Show me brushing."

Child: Child brushes his/her hair (with only as much help as needed to get it right).

Teacher immediately reinforces the correct response, and even more so if unprompted.

Most-to-Least Prompting ("Errorless Learning") and the Transfer Trial

Typically, a "transfer trial" would follow each prompted trial. This involves giving the child an opportunity to respond (and to be reinforced for responding) without being prompted, or with less of a prompt. You use the transfer trial to fade the prompt as quickly as possible so that the behaviour being taught does not become prompt-dependent. Most-to-Least Prompting (and the "transfer trial" which should follow each prompted trial) works very well and should be used with almost everything that you are trying to teach your child to do. The only general exception occurs when you reach the stage where it might actually benefit your child to experience some frustration – and that is not likely to be soon!

Mixing Easy and Difficult Tasks/Targets

One way to keep the value of working with you higher than either escape/avoidance or repetitive behaviour(s) is to have about four already-learned/easy teaching targets for every being-learned/more difficult target – and be sure to reinforce both effort and success. The point is to see that the child is receiving sufficient reinforcement[34] that he enjoys the experience and remains motivated to keep trying to learn. By the same token, the language that you use with your child should be about 75-80% declarative (i.e., narrative) to about 20-25% imperative. That is, no more than about 20-25% of your communications should be placing demands on your child. That might creep up a bit when doing instruction but, in that case, it has to be balanced with sufficient reinforcement to keep the learning enjoyable. The rest of your talking to him/her should be just for sharing information and enjoyment.

---

[34] Of course, once your child gets "on a roll" – on a learning roll, that is – the achievement itself will provide much of the needed reinforcement; and I have seen children respond (more-or-less correctly) to dozens of task demands with no other reinforcement than the enjoyment that they get from demonstrating their accomplishments, even when the teacher's approval is more implicit than explicit.

Mixing/Varying Targets and Tasks

This means switching among different kinds of tasks: motor imitation, echoics, requests/demands (mands), labels (tacts), intraverbals, and so on; and switching between tasks that require verbal communication and those that require nonverbal communication. You will learn what all of these new and strange terms mean in just a little while. Mixing/varying targets and tasks helps to reduce boredom and keep the child attentive.

Teaching to Fluency

Teaching to fluency involves taking an existing skill and increasing both its speed and accuracy to the point where it is actually useful to the child. That is, children need to be able to respond not only accurately, but quickly as well, since very few behaviors are truly functional when they occur with a long delay after the antecedent. For example, a child may be able to tell someone his name, but if he is not able to do so quickly – say he answers 10 seconds after being asked – he will have already lost the attention of the person asking, and that less-than-fluent name-answering skill isn't going to help his social success. The goal of fluency training for this child would be to increase his rate of performance of telling people his name until it became fast and accurate and therefore meaningful for the child within his social context.

Research has shown that teaching a skill to fluency (achieving accuracy <u>plus</u> speed as a requirement of mastery) achieves several goals, particularly Retention (The ability to recall the learned material on demand), Endurance (The ability of the skill to be performed at a particular level over time and in the presence of distractions), and Application (The ability to combine elements of a behavior to create a more sophisticated behavior).

To teach for fluency in responding during ABA-based instruction, the teacher needs to begin by controlling for two variables: (1) latency (the time between the antecedent and the child's response), and (2) intertrial intervals (the time between teaching trials)

The issue of latency is taken care of through most-to-least prompting ("errorless learning"). Intertrial intervals refer to the time between the end of the consequence for one trial and the beginning of the next antecedent. Short intertrial intervals may be accomplished in part by taking probe data as a way of checking for acquisition (rather than taking the time to record correctness of response after each teaching trial), thus allowing more teaching to be done in less time (and keeping distractibility and motivation-to-work high compared to anything else that the child might find to do) – remembering, of course, that you do need to take enough time to complete each trial before moving on to the next.

Having done that, it then becomes possible to carry out fluency-producing drills on the skills which are being learned (and to graph these results in such a way as to indicate whether or not the child has attained fluency in those particular skills – more about that later). Fluency-producing drills are carried out as follows:

- First, choose a specific learned skill which you wish to bring to fluency.
- Then, select a rate of responding that you would like the child to reach – this becomes the goal towards which your child is working for that particular skill.[35]
- Run short, sprint-type drills (as a general rule, shorter drills – even as short as 10 seconds in some cases – tend to be more effective than longer drills).
- Graph the results, using a separate graph for each skill that you are attempting to bring to fluency.[36] The graphs should show increased fluency with practice.

---

[35] Not everyone agrees that frequency goals should be established. It has been suggested, for example, that setting "frequency goals" or "frequency aims" for children with autism assumes that fluency is a function of attaining a certain frequency goal (or range) of responding, whereas neither skill acquisition nor skill retention is determined by any specific norms: Rate of response is related to retention, endurance and application of the knowledge learned, but the specific rate and/or celeration which will result in retention, endurance and application is unique to each child.

[36] There are no commonly recognized norms for performance standards, but you should be able to expect about one response per second over a 15 to 30 second period of time. Simple math skills can be targeted at slightly higher rates. The average Grade one student should aim for 60 to 100 words per minute reading words orally from a passage. Reading consonant and vowels sounds should aim for 80 to 120 per minute. Reading numbers should aim for 120 to 150 per minute. On the other hand, I wouldn't place too much credence in any of these suggested rates.

In a paper entitled Fluency: Achieving True Mastery in the Learning Process, Binder, Haughton and Bateman note that effective practice is the key to any fluency-based program:

- Effective practice always has a goal.[37]
- It is easier to attain fluency on small, achievable "chunks" or components of a larger performance than to attain mastery on the whole thing at once.
- For students who have not yet achieved fluency, practice for short intervals is generally more productive than practice for longer continuous time periods.
- Practice every day and keep a graphic record of learning progress on each specific type of skill.
- When performance shows little or no improvement and is below the aim, try working on a simpler task.

You can find materials which can be used to teach fluent responding (to certain language and visual cues, such as What color? What shape? or What Size?) at: www.autismteachingtools.com/page/bbbbfg/bbbbfz

Standard celebration charting of such frequency data, should you wish to add this refinement to your teaching repertoire, is discussed more fully later in this paper, under the heading of Data Recording Procedures.

More Effective Teaching Techniques That You Should Know

When parents are first teaching their children to speak, they begin by using language in the child's presence. Then they start to label objects in the environment for the child. They and their child see a bus and the parents say, "bus." They and their child see a truck and the parents say, "truck." What they are teaching their child, through this kind of pairing, is to associate the object with its label.

If they are fortunate and the child attempts to repeat the label after them – that is, if the child is echoic – they acknowledge the attempt, usually by either (1) repeating the child's vocalization or (2) providing the correct vocalization. For example, the parent sees a

[37] And that goal should always include ensuring retention, endurance and application of the skills being learned.

squirrel and draws it to the child's attention by pointing at it and enthusiastically saying, "Oh, look! A squirrel." Often, after many such pairings, the child attempts the word, and the attempt may be something like, "keo." That is when immediate reinforcement becomes crucial, usually with something like an enthusiastic, "Yes, it's a squirrel." Or the child may label (tact) a cat by saying "meow meow," and you respond with an enthusiastic "meow meow" or "Yes, the kitty says 'Meow, meow.'" [38]

This process is repeated and repeated and repeated and repeated until the child acquires, first, a repertoire of associations between objects and their labels and, second (if you are fortunate enough to have a child that will attempt the word), a vocal repertoire consisting of those labels for those objects.

Similarly, a beginning learner may ask for a drink by saying "Wa," and the parent acknowledges the effort by saying something like, "Water" (which models the correct response) and providing the drink of water, thereby reinforcing the child's request (with the water), pairing yourself with the reinforcement, and possibly even socially reinforcing the child's efforts to communicate.[39]

And Don't Forget About Generalization

Generalization refers to ensuring that learned behaviours are available to the child in a variety of settings, i.e., that things learned in one setting are not limited to that setting. For example, once the child begins learning to say "Cookie" when shown a cookie (or a picture of a cookie) by one instructor, it is important that he learn to do so when asked by a different person, in a different place, with a different kind of cookie, etc. Since generalization won't necessarily happen automatically, you should count on having to use multiple instructors, in different settings, etc.

At one time, generalization was thought of as a task separate from the initial teaching, something added on that could be done later. Now it is thought of as something which ought to be built into all of your teaching. The need for generalization is one of the reasons that it

---

[38] Remembering that having a label for an object is more important than having the correct label for that object. Later on, you can teach the correct label.

[39] And, of course, tangible reinforcement can always be used in the beginning if that works better for a particular child.

is essential for the parents to be involved in their child's teaching/learning, since they will have so many opportunities to contribute to it.

Skinner's Analysis of Language from a Functional Perspective

Most people think of language[40] as being either:

1) Receptive = understanding what someone else says
2) Expressive = being able to use language to make yourself understood

Some time ago, however, B.F. Skinner (1947) analysed language into its functional components (i.e., breaking it down into its uses). Here are a few examples:

Repeating something that has been seen or heard (Motor Imitation and Echoics)

Receptive identification of objects (Receptive ID)

Demanding/requesting (Mands)

Contacting or labelling (Tacts)

The language used to talk about something in its absence, such as "What colour is a fire truck?" The child responds, "Red!" (Intraverbals)

As it turns out, teaching language from a functional perspective has proven to be very productive.

Demanding/Requesting (Mands)

Typically, language proceeds from imitation through manding to labelling and intraverbals. A typical preschool child will make 500-1000 mands per day. Manding is usually taught before labelling because the reinforcer is built-in – the child is motivated to ask for things and reinforced by getting them – and is usually taught in the child's natural environment. When teaching manding, think "motivating operations." Ask yourself, "How am I going to arrange things so that [my child] is motivated to mand?"

At first, teach words that request (mand) reinforcers, e.g., particular foods or drinks, a particular toy, etc. And never teach only

---

[40] And remember that language can be vocal (i.e., spoken words) or non-vocal (i.e., picture exchange, signing, computer, etc.)

one mand at a time. Have several in acquisition at any given time. If teaching signing and the child has poor motor imitation, initially teach no more than 5-8 signs; if the child has moderate motor imitation, begin teaching up to 20 signs.

Always say (or, if you are teaching signing, sign and say) the name of the item three times as you deliver it, unless the child says (or signs) the word before you finish, in which case, deliver the item immediately.

In the beginning, don't try to teach words that look alike or sound alike. For example, the sign for eat and drink look very similar, the words eat and meat sound alike – you want to make it as easy as you can for your child to learn to communicate. Also, avoid teaching "general" words like "more," which can cause you immense problems when the child starts to use them indiscriminately.

Labelling (Tacts)

Typically, tacting begins with teaching the names (i.e., the labels or tacts) of those items which the child is motived to ask for, and may proceed through teaching the names of common object, common people, common actions, and body parts – other types of tacts can be found in curricula such as the ABLLS-R. In choosing what words to teach first, try to teach those that serve some purpose *for the child.* In fact, we should always be thinking about the functionality of what we are trying to teach. Ask yourself, "What purpose would it serve for my child to know this particular word?" That way, you will be capitalizing on the child's potential motivation to learn what you are trying to teach.

Receptive & Expressive Language by Feature, Function & Class

Receptive Language : "Touch cow."

Receptive Language by Feature, Function and Class: "Show me the one that says, 'Moo' " "Point to the one that gives us milk?" "Which one is an animal?"

Expressive Language by Feature, Function and Class (i.e., expecting a verbal response): "What does a cow say?" ('Moo?') "Which one gives us milk?" (from a number of animals) "And a cow is an…?" (animal)

Intraverbals

Intraverbals involve the ability to answer questions about something not present. Intraverbals play a major role in social interactions, usually in the form of answers to questions such as "How are you?" and "What did you do today?" The child's use of intraverbals typically grows out of being taught all the many associations of a word, including the named item's features, functions and the broader class to which it belongs.[41]

Once a child is able to identify and/or describe an object by its features, functions and class while the object is present, intraverbals are taught by teaching the same responses with the object absent (usually immediately afterwards). It is intraverbals that take language beyond rote learning and make it really useful.

Preschool Curricula

Ideas about specifically what to teach can be found in a variety of sources, including the following:

Teaching Language to Children with Autism or Other Developmental Disabilities by Mark Sundberg and James Partington (1998)

The Assessment of Basic Language and Learning Skills (the ABLLS-R) by James Partington (2006)

A Work in Progress by Leaf & McEachin (1999)

Relationship Development Intervention with Children, Adolescents and Adults by Gutstein & Sheely (2002)

Relationship Development Intervention with Young Children by Gutstein & Sheely (2002)

The RDI Book by Gutstein (2009)

---

[41] Patrick McGreevy has pointed out (in a workshop which I recently attended) that many of the things we teach serve no immediate purpose for the learner, and that we should at least consider functionality when deciding what to teach. This is particularly true for children and adults who are severely limited in what they can learn. For example, if you are teaching colours, you might consider teaching "red, yellow, and green" within the context of learning about traffic lights, and leave the other colours until the child has some particular use for them.

Social Skills Solutions: A Hands-On Manual for Teaching Social Skills to Children with Autism by Kelly McKinnon and Jane Krempa (2002)

Early Start Denver Model by Sally Rogers and Geraldine Dawson (2010)

Hawaii Early Learning Profile – Revised (VORT Corporation, 1994)

The Carolina Curriculum for Preschoolers with Special Needs by Nancy Johnson-Martin, Bonnie Hacker, and Susan Attermeier (2004)

The Goal Mine by Donald and Maureen Cahill (2003)

I tend to favour basing much (but not all) of any ABA program for a child with autism on the ABLLS-R, since it provides such a clear visual summary of the child's achievement across a wide variety of areas. However, with the more recent publication of the VB-MAPP and The RDI Book, I believe that it would be foolish to ignore the additional information which they contain – specifically:

(1) for the VB-MAPP, age-referenced assessment, barriers to learning, and recommendations regarding transition to a less restrictive learning environment than afforded by one-on-one instruction, and even whether it might not be a better curriculum around which to build your ABA program, as some practitioners seem to have found, and

(2) for the RDI Book, its detailed early social relating curriculum and suggestions about how that might be approached. In spite of the fact that it is not an ABA book, much of its instructional content can be reframed in ABA terms.

The ABLLS-R

The Assessment of Basic Language and Learning Skills (the ABLLS-R), by James Partington, assesses language from a functional perspective and can help you determine:

- what needs to be taught (i.e., a curriculum)[42]
- what are the small teachable steps
- what the child already knows
- what are the next steps in the curriculum

Completed every four to six months, it is also a good way to keep track of your child's progress.

For children who have very few skills, you can begin with a simpler form of the ABLLS, the Behavioral Language Assessment (BLA). Both of these assessment and program planning tools are by Mark Sundberg & James Partington and may be readily obtained from them through (www.behavioranalysts.com) or locally (i.e., in Ontario, where this book was written) through Parentbooks (416 537-8334). The BLA can be found in Teaching Language to Children with Autism or Other Developmental Disabilities by Mark Sundberg and James Partington (1998). The Assessment of Basic Language and Learning Skills - Revised) by James Partington is a separate publication, which comes as both a test and a scoring guide.

The ABLLS-R looks difficult but, if you do decide to use it, and you don't have to, you will find that it is really fairly simple. Remember that all you are trying to do is get some idea of what your child already knows and some ideas about what to teach next; it doesn't have to be a totally precise measure. Fortunately, you don't have to buy a new copy of the ABLLS-R each time you use it. You just add on what your child has learned since the last time you filled it out.

The VB-MAPP

Having developed a beginning individual service plan based on the ABLLS-R, I would modify it in two complementary ways: (1) with information derived from the VB-MAPP and (2) supplemented by a variety of social skills objectives such as those found in McKinnon and Krempa's "Social Skills Solutions."

---

[42] As a general rule, ABA programs for children with autism need to address a wide variety of areas of learning. The ABLLS-R includes items from 25 areas, and Jim Partington, its author, recommends that each of these areas be addressed in the child's program. Mary Barbera (the author of Verbal Behavior) has expressed a preference for about 20 or so teaching targets at any one time, and that each can be learned within one to two weeks. I tend to agree with these recommendations.

Social/Emotional Relating Skills

And this is where we come to Gutstein's Relationship Development Intervention (RDI):

Unfortunately, while useful and a very good place to start formal instruction,[43] the ABLLS-R is more about language than about social relationships. It is just as important to teach social/emotional relating skills as it is to teach language skills (and you have already made a good start on that through playing with your child). However, we are still learning how best to teach social relating, so we typically don't do as good a job of it as we do of teaching language.

Some people suggest that we never will, because children with autism lack the necessary connections within their brains. We don't believe that! Why? Because many children with autism do learn how to relate socially. However, for social/emotional relating skills, you will benefit from additional guides to instruction, as well as from teaching methods that place a greater emphasis on modelling than do most ABA programs. Operant conditioning has its place, but remember that ABA programs should be making use of everything that we know about how children learn, not just operant conditioning.

Many authors have written about social skills training (for example, see the previously suggested book list). This information about social skills training is especially important to ABA practitioners because research has shown that ABA-based programs do a better job of teaching communication than they do of teaching social skills.[44]

One of the most comprehensive social development programs is Gutstein's Relationship Development Intervention (RDI),[45] and much can be learned about the development of social/emotional relating

---

[43] Other sources of information about curriculum are listed elsewhere in this publication.

[44] Research conducted by ErinoakKids during its first year or so of providing intensive behavioural intervention, for example, found a fifteen month increase in communication skills in fifteen months, but an increase of only six months in social and daily-living skills during that same time. Of course, to put that in perspective, one-on-one intensive teaching is not the best venue in which to teach social skills, and "therapy" isn't necessarily the best place for teaching daily living skills.

[45] RDI is a rapidly evolving program – one recent publication (as of May 2005) is "Going to the Heart of Autism: The Relationship Development Intervention Program (2004), available as a DVD (see www.rdiconnect.com). I would also highly recommend Gutstein's The RDI Book (2009).

from examination of his website (www.rdiconnect.com) and publications. Recently, we have begun to see ABA service providers starting to incorporate RDI goals and teaching procedures into their ABA programs.

Gutstein's Relationship Development Intervention (RDI)

According to Gutstein, the sensory and processing difficulties present in individuals with autism spectrum disorders makes it hard for them to adapt well to rapidly changing situations. Change is more likely to be experienced as threatening than as exciting, with the result that individuals with ASD tend to prefer sameness, and to experience novelty as disruptive. Unfortunately (from a learning perspective), social situations are not simple and unchanging. To get along socially, you have to learn:

to "see things through your partner's eyes," [46]

to coordinate your actions with theirs,

to know when the two of you are not on the same track,

to know how to repair misunderstandings,

to learn to observe how others feel and, based on that information, to continually change your own behaviour so as to help keep them happy,

These skills are not easily learned by children with ASD. Fortunately for them and us, however, Gutstein has broken down the development of social/emotional relating into twenty-eight steps (see Gutstein's website for a more complete listing of the various steps in this developmental process):

Examples of beginning steps: emotion sharing, joint attention, social referencing and coordinating actions

---

[46] Many RDI concepts appear to be quite abstract when compared to the concrete behaviours being addressed by ABA approaches to the treatment of children with autism. However, as soon as you ask yourself, "What will I use as an indicator of success?" you will find yourself needing to choose concrete, observable behaviours to use as evidence that the "abstract" objective has been achieved. Thus, for anyone interested in tracking actual progress, the apparent RDI-abstract and ABA-concrete dichotomy disappears in actual practice.

Examples of intermediate steps: collaboration, joint attention, conversation, perspective taking

Examples of advanced steps: forming personal, family and group identities

Gutstein strongly advises that you not try to rush this process, on the grounds that doing so would only lead to short term gain and long term loss – each step needs to be well consolidated before moving on to the next one. It can take the better part of a year to even get beyond the first step or two in this process of learning to be a social human being, so don't get discouraged.

"Essential Elements" of any RDI program include, according to Gutstein:

- A thorough Relationship Development Assessment (see the RDA manual)
- Clear objectives based on this assessment
- Data collected daily and summarized weekly
- Program modifications based on this data.
- Parents adopt RDI as a lifestyle and primary (but not necessarily the only) intervention
- Consultants function as parent facilitators
- Dyads and groups are formed from peers matched by Relationship Development stage. Participants are not placed in peer dyads until they have mastered all of the Functions through Stage 8. Participants are not placed in small peer groups until they have mastered all of the Functions through Stage 10.
- Intervention plans include specific methods for developing episodic (i.e., autobiographical) memory, including previewing and reviewing experiences. RDI programs also include an emphasis on the development of relative thinking and executive functioning skills.
- Parents:
  - function as the primary coaches/facilitators

  - emphasize declarative communication
  - create frequent periods of "productive uncertainty" to provide the child with opportunities/motivation for referencing
  - rely on indirect prompts whenever possible
  - leave sufficient room in the daily schedule for experience sharing

- Relationship Development Intervention should be (according to Gutstein) carried out under the supervision of a qualified RDI consultant.

Gutstein is also trying to develop a model which will teach the 55% of communication that is

(1) nonverbal and

(2) so much a part of social relating.

Consequently, in addition to teaching parents to think in terms of establishing a master-apprentice relationship with their child, Gutstein is attempting to teach them to communicate with their child nonverbally (as well as verbally, of course).

Much of this instruction is based on modeling – reframing "instructional control" (a primarily reinforcement-based concept) as "a master-apprentice relationship" (a primarily modeling-and-reinforcement-based concept). In an effective master-apprentice relationship, it is the "master" (the adult) who teaches the "apprentice" (the child). To do so, the master has to have instructional control, but a master-apprentice relationship involves more than just the adult having instructional control. It also implies a commitment on the part of the adult to teaching the child, through a combination of modelling and reinforcement, the practicalities of living as an emotionally-relating person – which requires more of a commitment to interacting with the child than is usually required of the parents of most typically-developing children.

Many of these same techniques can be found in "More Than Words" and "The Autistic Spectrum Parents' Daily Helper." You can also expect to see them in any good ABA program, although perhaps not so formalized as in RDI.

Final Thoughts on Gutstein's RDI

RDI is a rapidly evolving approach to the treatment of autism, and what is true of it today may not be true of it tomorrow. RDI techniques/emphases that I would expect to see receiving greater emphasis in ABA programs in the near future include:

- the insistence on parental involvement in the child's program
- more attention to "dynamic" intelligence
- an increase in the use of declarative language
- more emphasis on social relating
- more attention to nonverbal communication
- increased "productive uncertainty" (so that the child looks to the instructor for guidance). Note that, to be "productive," the uncertainty has to be delivered in small enough doses that it is not overwhelming and gradually increases the child's tolerance for the fluidity typically encountered in social situation
- the use of photos and memory books to facilitate autobiographical memories

Where autism is concerned, we live in the best of times and the worst of times. It is the worst of times because the incidence of autism seems to be burgeoning. It is the best of times because our ability to address its challenges is developing by leaps and bounds. RDI, like Floortime, has much to contribute to this enterprise, and incorporating some of the insights and techniques derived from it can help to improve ABA-based instruction.

Reinforcement: A Brief Review

A consequence, reinforcement occurs immediately after the behaviour that it strengthens (Why immediately?). It can be the provision of something desirable such as a piece of cookie (positive reinforcement) or the removal of something undesirable such as noise (negative reinforcement). It is much harder to find appropriate negative reinforcers than it is to find appropriate positive reinforcers, so think "positive."

As a general rule, consequences that the child finds rewarding are going to be good reinforcers, although this is not always the case. And the only **sure** way to determine what will be reinforcing for the child is to present the consequence after the behaviour and see if the behaviour is strengthened – because that is how reinforcement is defined.

In choosing potential reinforcers, look for the following characteristics:

- Items that you can control access to
- Easy to deliver
- Available for a short duration or
- Easy to remove
- Can be delivered on multiple occasions
- Always seem to be motivating

The Reinforcement Value of Consequences Changes From Time to Time: The Role of Motivating Operations (Establishing Operations)[47]

You should know that the reinforcement value of any particular consequence will change from time to time. For example, a drink of pop is more likely to be reinforcing when a child is thirsty than after he/she has just had a big drink; access to a favorite videotape is likely to be more reinforcing if the child hasn't already watched it earlier in the day.

Events (including those things you do) that alter the reinforcement value of a consequence are called Motivating Operations (MO's or EO's). The use of MO's can often most productively be taught (i.e., to instructors) within the context of teaching the child to make requests (manding)... because teaching your child to use language to ask for the things that he/she wants will provide lots of opportunities to think about how you can motivate him/her to ask for things.

If a child wants something, he/she will usually do something to try to get it. Your child may, for example, lead you by the hand to whatever it is that he/she wants. You can learn to use that motivation to teach your child to ask for what he/she wants. For example, you could place a

---

[47] Glasberg (Functional Behavior Assessment for People with Autism), who has one of the best expositions of functional behaviour assessment that I have seen, feels that "establishing operations" are so important that the A-B-C sequence of behavioural learning events should be re-cast as EO-A-B-C.

favorite toy just out of reach, so that your child will be motivated to ask for your help to get it. You could give your child some ice cream and "forget" to provide him/her with a spoon, so that he/she is motivated to ask for a spoon. You could place favorite toys in transparent containers that he/she needs your help to open. And, of course, the reinforcement for asking for what he/she wants is getting what has been requested.

Which Brings Us Back to Shaping

Of course, your child's beginning attempts to use language to ask for things is not likely to be very precise. Any attempt to vocalize or sign, however, gives you a place to start, and you can always shape up that response over time. And remember, whatever you are working on, don't forget to encourage any language and/or social interaction that your child gives you.

When working on shaping, you want to have the behaviour that you are teaching sufficiently well established that it doesn't have to be reinforced every time it occurs, before you raise the requirements for its being reinforced. Then, you want to raise your criteria for reinforcement in small enough steps that the child always has a fairly good chance of his behaviour being reinforced on any particular attempt. Remember, reinforcement is one of the most important keys to learning.

Don't complicate the learning task unnecessarily by requiring a change (i.e., improvement) in more than one aspect of the behaviour at a time. And try not to correct mistakes from the antecedent side of the antecedent-behaviour-consequence sequence. You should think Reinforcement before thinking Antecedent, and try to let the child learn, from his/her own experience, which behaviours get reinforced and which don't. This seems to be very hard for parents to do!

And try not to correct the child's mistakes (e.g., misbehaviours) by using aversive consequences; learning goes faster without aversives. If you miscalculate and the child's behaviour deteriorates, drop back to an easier stage in the process, and work your way up again. Then, when the behaviour has been shaped up to your satisfaction, build it into the child's everyday repertoire, continuing to reinforce it from time to time until it becomes reinforced by the environment's naturally occurring consequences.

Now, Let's Talk a Bit More about Undesirable Behaviours

Children who have trouble learning language tend to learn other, often undesirable, behaviours instead. These undesirable behaviours usually persist because the child is intermittently rewarded (i.e., rewarded once in a while) for them, but sometimes because the child is intermittently punished for them.

Dangerous behaviours need to be prevented. Other undesirable behaviours should be ignored if possible, because they are often being strengthened by the attention that they receive – but you have to be entirely consistent, otherwise you find yourself intermittently encouraging the behaviour that you don't want to get. Behaviours that are consistently ignored tend to die out (also known as "extinction"); behaviours that are intermittently reinforced tend to become resistant to extinction.

One of the best ways to get rid of undesirable behaviours is to teach (and reward the child for) desirable behaviours that are incompatible with them, e.g., language, compliance, waiting, frustration tolerance, transitions, and so on. Increasing the overall amount of reinforcement in the child's life also helps to eliminate undesirable behaviours, although you still have to be entirely consistent in not rewarding (or punishing) the child for those undesirable behaviours.

Of course, if undesirable behaviours are sensory-sensitivity-related, you will want to take that into account. That is, the child's undesirable behaviours may be being maintained by either hypo- or hyper-sensitivity-related reinforcement (such as escape from over-stimulation), and you may want to accommodate to your child's sensory needs as best you can and/or carry out a desensitization process before starting to think in terms of other kinds of reinforcement.

A Couple of Final Points on Behavioural Issues: First, don't forget about "shaping" – you can always reinforce any movement in the direction of the kind of behaviour that you want the child to learn. Second, remember that undesirable behaviours usually serve a purpose for the child, and understanding that purpose is often the key to eliminating the behaviour. This may require what is called a "functional analysis" [48] of the child's undesirable behaviours.

---

[48] Glasberg's recent book, "Functional Behavior Assessment for People with Autism" is an excellent primer on the subject.

Functional Analysis of Behaviour

A functional analysis of the child's behaviour consists of information-gathering that results in a hypothesis about the function(s) that the behavior is serving for the child. It starts with observation of the circumstances in which the problem behaviour occurs, to try to identify the antecedents (i.e., the "triggers") and the consequences (i.e., the reinforcers that are maintaining the behavior). These reinforcers are likely to be one or more of the following:

Attention

Escape or avoidance of some task(s)

Escape or avoidance of some social situation

Access to a preferred item or desired activity

The sensory stimulation provided by repetitive behaviours.

This information then serves as the basis for developing a plan of action that modifies environmental factors and/or consequences while providing instruction in (and reinforcement of) new, more appropriate behaviors. Throughout this process, data is collected and evaluated, and ongoing revisions are made to your plan of action (your "Behavior Intervention Plan") based upon analysis of that data.

Arbitrary and Natural Consequences

Reinforcement can be either the natural consequence of a behaviour or an arbitrary or contrived consequence, i.e., one devised by the instructor. Most reinforcers used in ABA, except for social approval and achievement, are arbitrary. Natural reinforcers have a better chance of maintaining the behaviour over the long haul. (Why?)

Fortunately, at some point in the learning process, language, social interaction and social approval/praise can become enjoyable for the child and, therefore, likely to be reinforcing in and of themselves. At that point, the instructor doesn't have to keep reinforcing language and social behaviours with arbitrary consequences, such as toys and edibles, in order for the child to continue to engage in them.

Arbitrary aversive consequences (such as spanking and/or yelling at the child) interfere with the learning of behaviours that you may want to teach (e.g., as a substitute for any undesirable behaviours that you want to get rid of), so don't use them! Instead, think of teaching (through reinforcement) the behaviours that you want to get.

Reinforcement: Continuous and Intermittent

Reinforcement can occur in response to every instance of a behaviour (a continuous reinforcement schedule) or less frequently (an intermittent reinforcement schedule). Moving from a continuous reinforcement schedule to an intermittent one is known as "thinning the reinforcement schedule."

Behaviour that is maintained through intermittent reinforcement is less susceptible to extinction (i.e., being forgotten/dying out when the reinforcement stops coming regularly) than behaviour that has received only continuous reinforcement. Therefore, thin the reinforcement schedule as opportunity permits (but not so much that the behaviour you are trying to teach is no longer worth the effort to the child.)

A Few More General Teaching Procedure Reminders

Always start each teaching session by pairing yourself with reinforcement, then gradually fade in the number of demands and, starting with easy tasks, gradually work your way up to more difficult tasks. Whenever possible let extinction (e.g., ignoring) and competing positive behaviours (and their reinforcers) take care of any problem behaviours that show up to interfere with the child's learning.

Augmentative Communication Systems

Both signing and PECS (Picture Exchange Communication System) provide a way to communicate that doesn't require the ability to vocalize. They are not mutually exclusive! Both have been used as stepping stones to speech, i.e., many children begin with PECS or signing and end up by talking. Initially, reinforce any speech that you get, since speech is such a superior way of communicating. Personally, I prefer signing over PECS, since the child can learn to do more with it if he/she has a cooperative audience.

Teaching to the Child's Preferred Sensory Modality

Many children with autism are visual learners, e.g., they can follow directions presented in picture form when they can't follow spoken instructions, or they learn best through watching. Some, however, are auditory learners – they need to hear it before it makes any sense to them. Some children need to do to learn, i.e., they are kinesthetic learners. Try to take advantage of whichever of these strengths the child has.

Chaining

Some behaviours, such as using the toilet, require that a number of steps be learned (Determining these steps is called doing a task analysis). Then you "chain" these steps together. One way to do this is to teach the first step in the procedure first, helping the child with all of the other steps in the process. Then, when that first step has been mastered, teach the second step, and so on. This is known as forward chaining.

Another way to teach these steps is to teach the last step in the procedure first, helping the child with all of the other steps in the process. Then, when that last step has been mastered, teach the second last step, and so on. This is known as backward chaining. Backward chaining is good when reinforcement comes at the end of a series of steps, as in many self-help skills. With backward chaining, the child may learn the intermediate steps before you even get to teach them, if you get lucky. Many skills, however, do not lend themselves to backward chaining. For example, you can't easily learn to ride a bike by learning the dismount first. In such cases, consider using forward chaining if chaining is needed.

"Scrolling"

Scrolling is the child's attempt to obtain reinforcement by offering you a variety of behaviours which have led to reinforcement in the past, not realizing that the reinforcement was given, not for the behaviour itself, but for the behaviour as a response to a particular antecedent event (i,.e., as a response to a particular discriminative stimulus or cue).

Correction Procedures for Scrolling Procedure

1. Turn away, wait 2-3 seconds.

2. Re-present the antecedent.
3. Prompt immediately.
4. Fade prompts as quickly as possible on subsequent trials.

Example of Correction Procedure for Scrolling

Instructor shows item and says, "What do you want?"

Child: Chips, popcorn, movie…

Instructor removes item (if visible), turns away and comes back with item.

Instructor shows item and says, "What do you want?" and immediately names item

From here on, teaching proceeds as usual.

A Few More Correction Tips

Do not prompt when a child has just made a mistake or is in the middle of making a mistake. No more than three corrections should be done on an incorrect response. End on an errorless, prompted trial (if the child doesn't get it right without prompting before then) and then move to items on which the child has a high probability of being correct. You can always come back to that item later. Whenever possible, end on the child's most independently successful response.

Data Recording Procedures: Probe Data [49]

Some instructors record correctness-of-response data after every single trial. Others do a quick check at the beginning of the session, to determine whether or not the child has retained the previously-learned items being probed.[50] More and more instructors are moving towards recording probe data rather than recording the correctness of the child's answers after every trial. This allows for more teaching to be done.

---

[49] See the discussions of probe data in the Mariposa School's Employee Training Manual, which may be downloaded for free from www.mariposaschool.org and on Christina Burk's website, www.ChristinaBurkABA.com

[50] And continue to check periodically, to ensure that mastered skills are being retained over time, i.e., that they continues to be mastered; and if you find that any previously-learned skill has been lost, be sure to put it back onto "acquisition" again.

Have a list of items to check, to see if they have been learned. The process of taking probe data should look as much like an actual teaching session as possible: mixing easy and difficult tasks, etc. If the correct response is given quickly and accurately and with sufficient volume, record a YES. Otherwise, record a NO. If NO, prompt to correct the response and move on to the next trial.

Data Recording Procedures: Graphing/Charting:[51]

"A picture is worth a thousand words? - B. Taylor

Graphing (also known as charting) your child's progress gives you a really handy way of determining at a glance just how well your teaching program is working, and it is an important part of every ABA program!! Unfortunately, for many of the service providers who work with our children, representing data graphically seems to be more difficult than I think it ought to be – hence this brief introduction.

A graph is a visual representation of how behaviour change has occurred over time. Graphing behaviour change makes it easier to compare the levels of the target behaviour before (baseline), during (treatment) and after (generalization/maintenance) intervention. The direction or slope of the data path over time, also referred to as the trend line, will indicate whether the behaviour is increasing or decreasing (i.e., whether or not a particular skill is being acquired or lost), as well as the rate of change being observed.

Components of a Graph

Seven components are necessary for a graph to be complete:

- **Graph Title**: Each graph should be accurately and concisely labelled with a title that captures the behaviour being targeted, e.g., number of requests per hour.
- **Labels for x axis and y axis**: the y axis (vertical axis) usually tells you the target behaviour and the dimension of measurement, e.g., Cumulative # of tacts acquired; Number of

---

[51] Thanks to Diane Sardi, BCABA, for her assistance with this data recording section.

head hits, etc. The x axis (horizontal axis) usually reflects the unit of time, e.g., days, weeks.

- **Numbers or scale on x axis and y axis**: The numbers along the x and y axes should accurately capture and reflect the range within which the target behaviour is changing.
- **Data Point**: Data points must be plotted correctly to indicate the changing status of the target behaviour. Data points are connected to form a data path which will assist in visually identifying the trend line, or rate of behaviour change.
- **Phase Lines**: a phase line is a vertical line that is drawn on the graph to depict when a change in circumstance has occurred, e.g., sickness, a holiday, an increase in difficulty of the task, a change in the instruction, etc. The change can be from baseline to treatment, between conditions such as intervention phase and generalization phase, or to depict the different steps of a particular program. For example, one could be graphing # of probes to mastery in each step of a backward chained task analysis of hand washing – water off, rinse soap off hands, rub hands together, get soap on hands, turn water on, etc. Each step would be demarked by a phase change line, and data points across phases would not be connected. Each phase line can, and often needs to be, labeled to indicate what change in circumstance occurred.
- **Phase Labels**: Each phase depicted on a graph should be labeled at the top of the graph, above the particular phase.
- **Legend**: A legend that tells what each data path represents (since line graphs can display more than one data set at a time, and the legend tells which line represents which set of data). When only one set of data points is being plotted on the graph, no separate legend is required, since the label on the vertical axis should identify the data being plotted.

The following graphs illustrate some of these principles.

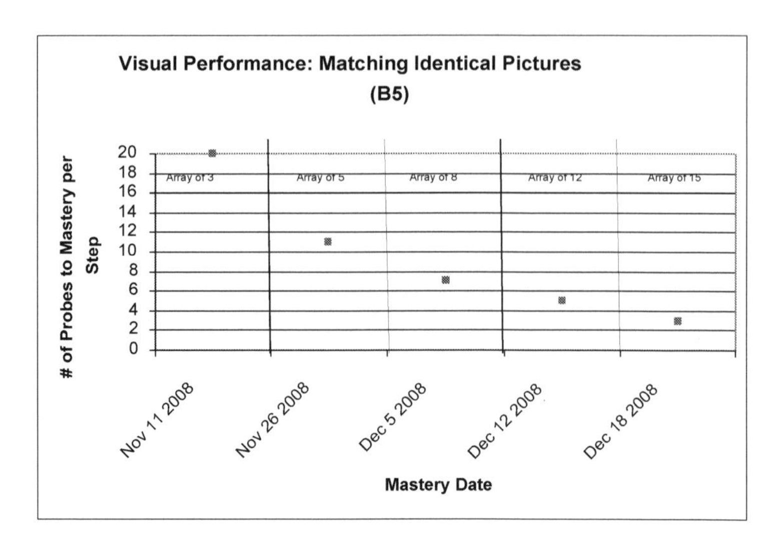

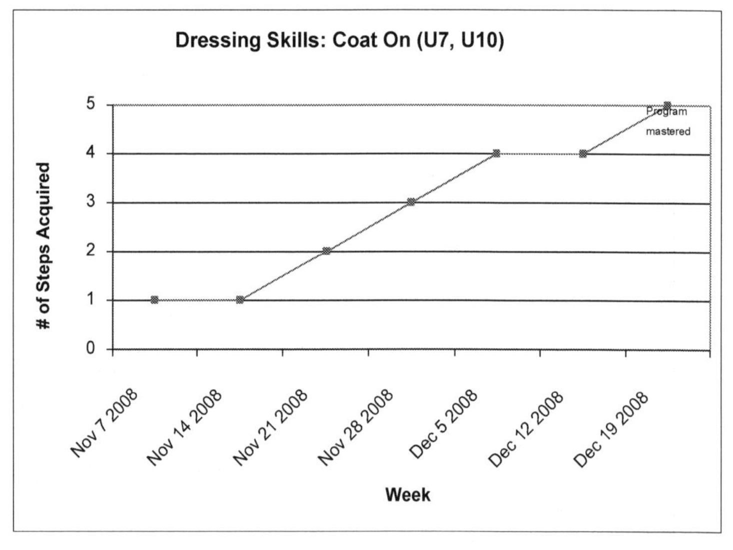

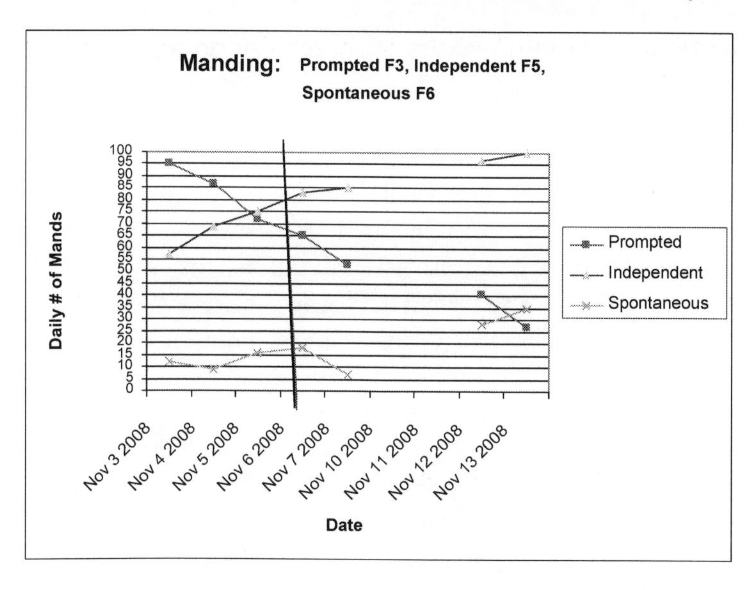

Note that the slope of the trend line in the first (Visual Performance: Matching Identical Pictures) and third of these graphs (Manding: Prompted F3, Independent F5, Spontaneous F6) can be a bit misleading, if you don't happen to be paying attention, because the time between data points in these two graphs is not uniform – if the time between data points were uniform, the slope of the data paths would be different than shown in these two graphs.

Note also that when a line is drawn connecting the data points, it forms the data path. A data path indicates continuity in the data collection process. If there is a break in the expected sequence of intervention – vacation, Christmas holidays, the child was sick, or the teaching target was changed (e.g., from finding a picture in an array of three items to finding a picture in an array of six items) – put a break in the data path and indicate on the graph just what the disruption was.

Celeration and Celeration Charting

One further point: As a general rule, we are not only concerned about ensuring that the child is learning. We are also concerned about helping the child to learn how to learn. That "learning how to learn" should be reflected in a trend line that demonstrates acceleration in the rate at which skills are being acquired – the child's acquisition of new skills should be seen to be accelerating over time rather than just increasing over time. The type of graphing which best captures such acceleration in learning is known as "celeration charting" (a term chosen to represent the kind of graphing that makes it easy to determine acceleration and/or deceleration of skill acquisition).

In the case of Celeration Charting, you chart the number of items correct within some particular period of time, e.g., during a ten second interval recorded each hour, during a five minute interval recorded every teaching session, etc., rather than just charting either the number or percentage of items correct. This is done using a specially-designed logarithmic graph paper known as the "Standard Celeration Chart") (See the Handbook of the Standard Celeration Chart, Deluxe Edition, by Pennypacker, Gutierrez and Lindsley (2003), published by the Cambridge Centre for Behavioral Studies and available from the CCBS Store at www.behavior.org).[52]

In my opinion, while any kind of charting is good, Celeration Charting[53] is important enough that it should be part of the skill set of all ABA providers – I am told that it has been on the CBCA exam, for those of you who wish to obtain this ABA-proficiency certification – and while the Standard Celeration Chart looks more complicated, it is said to be so simple that even six years olds can easily learn it and teach it to others. Furthermore, it has the added bonus of being more useful than charting on ordinary graph paper since, if the child's program is set up properly, the child's rate of acquisition of new knowledge (as indicated by his or her performance on the tasks being taught) should accelerate over even short periods of time, up to some reasonable goal – and even a glance at the chart will tell you whether

---

[52] How to use a celeration chart is well-illustrated by John Eshleman at members.aol.com/standardcharter/learnpix.html

[53] A how-to-chart manual by Rick Kubina can be found
at http://www.precisionteachingresource.net/chartoverview.pdf
and one by Carl Binder at http://www.binder-riha.com/Binder_ISPI2004_Charting.pdf
Should you be interested in pursuing this topic further, see www.celeration.org and the following internet resources:
www.celeration.net
www.fluency.org *and* www.fluency.org/MeasurementCounts_Links.html
members.aol.com/standardcharter
www.chartshare.net
seahorse.mma.edu/~sarna/index.html *and* seahorse.mma.edu/~sarna/sprints.html
www.teonor.com/ptdocs
psych.athabascau.ca/html/387/OpenModules/Lindsley
home.wi.rr.com/penzky/pt.htm
www.teachyourchildrenwell.ca/Home/mainpage.htm

or not that is happening. Additional advantages listed by Cancio & Maloney (1994) include a set of decision rules for what to do in response to the observed trend line, i.e., making a change in teaching strategy if the graph indicates that (1) the celeration line is less than had previously been projected, (2) the minimum acceleration is less than X 1.25, (3) correct responses are decelerating, (4) error responses are accelerating, or (5) the child's performance has been at your teaching goal for a couple of days.

Transition to School

In addition to guiding the child's IBI program, it is important that each Individual Service Plan link the child and family to a range of appropriate services and service providers in the community which, with parental consent, may be called upon to advise and participate in elements of a the child's Individual Service Plan. These providers might include:

- speech/language pathologist;
- teacher and/or principal;
- occupational therapist and/or physiotherapist;
- recreation staff;
- respite workers;
- counselors;
- home visitors;
- special services at home staff;
- special needs resource staff; and
- child care staff.

Each child's Individual Service Plan should clearly document the role of the family and these other service providers as they relate to the child's transition into the school system.

Service providers are expected to coordinate planning for the child's discharge/transition from intensive behavioural intervention and entry into the school system. Well in advance of discharge from the IBI program, whoever is assigned the transition coordination function (in most cases, this would be the child's Senior Therapist) is expected to:

- Prepare a summary that identifies the child's current strengths and weaknesses;
- Provides information about the child's participation in the IBI program (including the current state of language, social and academic skills needed to support successful school entry);
- Ascertain, with the parents and others, how and by whom the child's needs across domains may best be met on a continuing basis;
- Ensure that the family is either connected with (or referrals have gone in for) services that may be required after discharge from the IBI program and that they have a support network in place, and;
- Ask the parent(s)/caregiver(s) to arrange a case conference with the school and other professionals involved with the child to establish the school's priorities for successful integration, and to clarify the roles and responsibilities of those who will be involved with the child following discharge from the IBI program.

In addition, it is important for the Transition Plan to:

- Provide opportunities for community and school personnel to observe and discuss the child's IBI program – either in person or on video – to become familiar with the techniques used and the child's responses;
- Familiarize the family and child as to what to expect when starting school or transitioning to the community (e.g., rehearsing important routines that the child will have to know such as toileting, putting coats and shoes away); visiting the school or community placement to become familiar with the setting; introducing the child to the relevant people at the school or community placement, and; establishing transportation routines.

Obviously, the time required for these transition planning and coordination tasks, like program supervision, would be in addition to the ABA-based instruction that comprises the bulk of the child's IBI program.

Note that, in your child's program, you should (1) prioritize school readiness skills in the 6-12 months before school entry – nonacademic skills take precedence: attention, compliance, toilet training, etc. – and (2) consolidation/generalization of already learned skills, ensuring that IBI isn't the only place the child can demonstrate what he/she has learned. The goal of IBI is a smooth transition to a less intensive teaching situation, not abandonment by his or her IBI team.

Alert the school to your child's specialness in February for a September start date. And remember: Try to work on win-win collaboration with the school. They aren't your enemies. You might read "You're Going to Love This Kid!" by Paula Kluth (and, if you can afford it, buy a copy for the teacher).

Preschool and Kindergarten

Many daycare and nursery school settings, and some regular and private school settings will allow a "shadow" to assist your child to learn (1) to play, (2) to play with other children and (3) to learn that setting's routines. Typical Preschool and Kindergarten activities include Circle Time (weather, news, etc.), blocks and building, arts and crafts (often with a seasonal theme), pretend play centres, dress-up and role-play, and toy play. In classroom settings, incidental learning typically includes greetings, following classroom routines, staying within the boundaries of an area, listening in group, turn taking, sharing, imitating others, simple action songs, following simple instructions, looking to adults for guidance, transitioning from one activity to another, toileting, dressing and undressing skills, participating in cleanup, working and playing semi-independently, and some academic skills such as recognizing numbers, letters, colours and shapes.

When Your Child is Ready to Start School: Developing an Individual Education Program

Remember that the schools (in Ontario, at least) are not required to provide either expert ABA or an Educational Assistant for your child. They are, however, required to meet his/her needs. If your child is exceptional in any way, e.g., has autism, the school must develop an Individual Education Program (IEP) for him/her, as one of the first steps in meeting your child's needs. In some jurisdictions (again using Ontario as an example) an Identification, Placement and Review Committee (IPRC) meeting will be needed to identify your child as exceptional, to identify his strengths and needs, and to determine his/her placement, e.g., in a regular or segregated class. The IPRC sets the stage for, and formalizes, the school's the Individual Education Plan (IEP) for your child. The IEP, however, can be (and, in my opinion, should be) developed before the IPRC meeting.

A parent's main contribution to the IEP is likely to be to help identify his/her child's strengths, needs (teaching targets), accomplishments, teaching strategies that have proven to be effective, and any accommodations that are likely to be required. You should try to provide this information to the school two or three months before your child actually starts school, so that the teacher has something to work with until the school has time to develop, with you, an IEP for your child. You might note that the ABLLS-R provides a good summary of most of the skills required for successful school integration (as well as for immediate program planning). It has been adopted by many providers for use in the programs that they deliver, and it is being considered for use by many school boards. It can be helpful to you in designing your child's Individual Service Plan (ISP), and that may prove to be helpful when it is time to design your child's IEP – if your child's Individual Service Plan (ISP) "just happens" to use the same format as the school uses for its Individual Education Plan (IEP), it will contain most of the required information and may be useful to the school in developing your child's IEP.

The process of developing an IEP is spelled out in detail on the website of the Ontario Ministry of Education:
http://www.edu.on.ca/eng/general/elemsec/speced/iepeng.pdf

How to Organize and Manage an ABA Program

Although many parents are not going to have to manage their own child's ABA program, they should still know what is involved in doing so. Knowing what is involved in organizing and managing an ABA program will allow you to either set up your own program or to keep track of the program designed and managed by someone else for your child.

Steps in Getting an ABA Program Up and Running

- Get your hands on a curriculum such as the ABLLS-R.
- Determine what your child already knows.
- Set up a lesson area.
- Get start-up supplies.

- Draw up an Individual Service Plan
- Set up the curriculum binder
- If you possibly can, hire someone who knows how to deliver an ABA program – this way, i.e., as described in this primer!
- Hire and train other instructional staff.

Getting Your Hands on a Curriculum and Determining What Your Child Already Knows

These two items have already been addressed earlier in this discussion. Please refer to the appropriate sections of this paper for a review of that information.

Setting Up a Lesson Area

You will need a space that you can set up as an instructional area. Initially, it should be relatively free of distractions. You will need a child-sized table and chairs. There should be a play area; and play stations can be helpful, e.g., a trampoline, possibly a water play area, etc. You will need shelves and bins for storage of supplies. You will need room for any larger toys, etc. You will need wall space on which to display programs and other materials. A small television and a DVD or VCR would be very useful. You may need to child-proof the room. If you get an opportunity, visit a nursery school, kindergarten, and/or other ABA program to see how they organize things.

Getting Startup Supplies

Reinforcers (actually, potential reinforcers):

Food – pieces of cookie, chips, etc.

Drink – water, pop, juice, etc.

Sensory Stimulation – cuddles, tickles, bouncing, swinging, music, etc.

Toys and other preferred activities.

Common objects (or toys objects) and pictures of common objects. These can be obtained from any of the usual toy stores.

Consider purchasing a set of the Language Builder Picture Cards available from Different Roads to Learning (www.difflearn.com), or the equivalent.

Get a 3-hole punch binder in which to keep records of programs and progress.

Set Up a Curriculum Binder

Typically, a Curriculum Binder contains:

- A list of current and mastered teaching targets.
- Lesson summaries/communication log.
- Program tracking sheets.
- A section for each part of the curriculum, e.g., fine and gross motor skills, mands, tacts, intraverbals, play skills, social skills, daily living skills, etc., etc.
- Graphs
- Notes

Drawing Up an Individual Service Plan

When your exceptional child reaches school age, the school will need to develop an Individual Education Plan (IEP) for him. As mentioned above, if you set up your Individual Service Plan (ISP) so that it can be used as the basis for his/her IEP, that will make life easier for both you and the school.

It is recommended that your ISP contain the following information;

- Basic identifying information.
- A summary of the child's exceptionalities, including any relevant medical and assessment information.
- A clear and specific statement of the child's strengths and needs.[54]

[54] Note that weaknesses are not the same as needs – children do not need their weaknesses. Weaknesses should indicated barriers to learning that need to be acknowledged and may have to be addressed.

- The child's current level of achievement in all relevant areas of development. (Note: You could use the ABLLS-R to help document this if you wish.)
- Goals for the next twelve or so months.
- Intermediate objectives or teaching targets as steps along the way.
- A general statement about how progress will be monitored.
- Indicators of achievement for each objective.
- Data collection, analysis and presentation (e.g., graphing) procedures.
- Reinforcers which have been found to be useful with this child, e.g., preferred activities.
- Teaching accommodations and resources required.
- Provision for maintenance and functionality of the behaviours being taught (including generalization, endurance, applicability and stability across situations).
- Planning for transition to the next setting. This should be written in right from the beginning.
- Instructors and their respective responsibilities.
- Responsibilities of other professionals with respect to the child's program.
- Role and responsibilities of the parents in the child's program.
- Level of intensity and settings for the instruction.

Other important points to consider in developing an ISP:

- There should be a schedule for review of the ISP.
- The ISP should be dated.
- The ISP should be signed off on by the parents and by the person supervising the program.
- All concerned have a copy of the program.

Please keep in mind that an ISP is much more comprehensive than just a list of objectives/teaching targets! Don't settle for anything less than a comprehensive plan for the remediation of your child's educational challenges.

Finding Someone to Help Supervise Your Child's Program

If at all possible, find a psychologist or a member of one of the other Regulated Health Professions who is knowledgeable about ABA (e.g., someone with BCBA credentials) and autism to oversee your child's program. Hire a senior or lead instructor – preferably BCBA certified – to design and supervise the day-to-day operation of the program (or you will have to do this job yourself, and there is a lot involved in it). Hire one or more trained instructors (or arrange for their training).

Hiring and Training Other Staff and Volunteers

Here are a few suggestions:

If you are going to be the one responsible for hiring and training your instructors, purchase the Help Us Learn materials: Training Manual and Program Manager's Guide.

Download the Mariposa School's Employee Training Manual (for Verbal Behaviour) from www.mariposaschool.org

Try to attend an introductory workshop by Carbone, McGreevy, Sundberg, Partington, or one of their associates.

Require that each of your instructors obtain and read Educate Toward Recovery and The RDI Book.

Screening Staff and Volunteers

Try to find staff and volunteers who have experience working with children. Be aware that, statistically, children who are developmental challenged are more likely to be physically and/or sexually abused than are normally developing children. Require potential staff and volunteers to provide you with a Police Check – you can offer to pay for it if you wish – and don't forget to have the Sex Offender Registry included in the police checks.

Obligation to Report

On the other side of the coin, you should also be aware that professionals working with your child may be obliged by law to report to a Children's Aid Society any cases of observed or suspected child abuse or neglect. For example, if the instructor arrives at your house and finds that you have gone out and left a young child alone, s/he may be required by law to report that incident to a Children's Aid Society (as is the case in Ontario).

A Few More Things to Remember

It can be very difficult having someone in your home almost every day, for extended periods of time. Having staff working with your child will be almost like having one or more additional adults as part of your family. However, staff are neither family nor friends – their relationship with you is a professional relationship, similar to the relationship that your child's teacher will have with you when your child starts attending school.

Managing Your Child's Program [55]

- Read the daily lesson summaries in the communication log.
- Chart your child's progress towards each of his or her teaching objectives.
- Meet with your treatment team regularly to update objectives.
- Move mastered items to generalization and maintenance.
- Have each instructor demonstrate their teaching for the others, in an attempt to get consistency among your staff.

Sample Team Meeting Outline

- Review current targets for successes and problems, and troubleshoot the problems.

---

[55] In Teaching Individuals with Developmental Delays, Lovaas lists eleven "Preparatory Steps," treatment guidelines that transcend specific teaching techniques. They include learning how to teach, realizing that improvement is slow, conquering guilt, forming a treatment team, learning how to manage your team, learning how to train your team, being careful not to be misled about treatment outcomes, not allowing the inherent demands placed on parents by intensive behavioural treatments to jeopardize your marriage or your relationship with other children in the family, entering your child in school after he/she has mastered the appropriate imitative, self-help, and language skills, building confidence and self-esteem, and having a thorough grasp of the basic principles of Applied Behaviour Analysis.

- Check for problematic behaviours and troubleshoot them. Think functional analysis!
- Give each instructor a teaching task to demonstrate.
- Check for consistency among instructors.
- Add new teaching targets, if necessary, and make sure they are clear.
- Discuss any scheduling issues.

Nurturing Your Staff and Volunteers

Wise parents nurture their staff and volunteers. Reinforce both general and specific desirable behaviours – remember their birthdays and anniversaries, provide snacks for meetings, let them know how important they are to you and your child, etc. Pay your staff on time. They aren't in it just for the money, but money definitely helps.

Your Role in Teaching Your Child

Whether or not you are the person primarily responsible for directing or delivering your child's ABA program, you must be involved in teaching him or her!! Learn the principles of ABA and apply them in all your interactions with your child. "What does that mean, exactly?" you may ask. Well, let's review what ABA is all about:

Determine what the child already knows.

Break the material to be learned into relatively small steps.

Starting where the child is, teach the next steps in each part of the curriculum

Measure the change.

Modify your procedures and goals as necessary to ensure continuing progress.

And how, specifically, do you teach these small, observable steps?

Begin by pairing your self with events which the child finds enjoyable, until you have established your (secondary) reinforcement value. Then think about using modeling and reinforcement to teach your child.

- **A**ntecedent Conditions – something that happens just before, and serves as a cue for, the behaviour that you want the child to learn (also called the Discriminative Stimulus or S^D).
- **B**ehaviour (something that the child does in Response to the antecedent conditions).
- **C**onsequences which increase the likelihood of occurrence of that behaviour when the child is presented with that particular Antecedent. (Such consequences are said to reinforce, or to be a reinforcer for, the behaviour that they follow).

Setting the Stage for Success

Expose your child to lots of language and fun things that you do together. Pair your praise and encouragement with the delivery of reinforcement so that social approval becomes reinforcing in itself. Do this a lot at first, and then continue to do it intermittently. Remember shaping: Reinforce any movement your child makes in the direction of doing what you want him/her to learn to do. And finally, a couple more teaching procedure reminders: Always start each interaction/teaching session by pairing yourself with reinforcement, then gradually fade in the number of demands and, starting with easy tasks, gradually introduce a few slightly more difficult, being-learned tasks; and whenever possible let extinction and competing positive behaviours (and their reinforcers) take care of any problem behaviours that show up to interfere with the child's learning.

A Few Effective Teaching Procedures

- Use "Most-to-Least" prompting.
- Think "Transfer Trial" – a transfer trial is an opportunity to respond without being prompted. (It is provided after a prompted response)
- Mix easy and difficult tasks.
- Mix/vary targets and tasks.
- And eventually, teach to fluency.

Now, Here Are a Few Tips for Surviving the Process

Preserve a part of your life for yourself. Shut everything down by 9 p.m. Children in bed, etc. Go out once a week, after your child goes to bed. Try to get away for a day or two a couple of times each year. Call on community support services as much as you need to.

Please remember that none of us is a perfect instructor (myself included). We all make mistakes, and that is all right. We all have the opportunity of getting better with practice. Children don't learn overnight. It takes lots of repetition for most things to be learned. Parents don't learn overnight, either, so don't be too hard on yourself if you fall short of perfection. It is hard work, but do try to have fun interacting with your child. That is as important as anything else you might accomplish.

Beyond ABA

Finally, I would like to remind you once again that there are other-than-ABA approaches to treating autism – ABA, the application of what we know about applying research-based knowledge of effective teaching procedures, is not the only approach to the treatment of autism. Some of that material is referenced on the ICDL website, but I might mention a few other sources of information as well. Jenny McCarthy's recent book, Louder Than Words, talks about her own journey through DAN! (Defeat Autism Now!) medical approaches to issues such as "yeast overgrowth, food and environmental allergens, mineral depletion and absorption issues, parasite or bacteria imbalance, metal toxicity," and diet. Then, because many children with autism also exhibit attentional problems, you might want to address that directly, either as part of your ABA program – Barbara Sher's book, Attention Games, can be a helpful resource for teaching a child to learn to focus – or through neurofeedback, hemoencephalographic feedback, Audio-Visual Entrainment, or even the use of Bate's Neuroliminal Brain Training CD (which I have heard of but with which I have no personal experience). However, these essentially non-ABA approaches are more-or-less outside of the scope of this particular introduction, although they do also make use of learning principles.

RMR December 2010

References

Abrams, P. and Henriques, L. (2004). The Autistic Spectrum *Parents' Daily Helper*: A Workbook for You and Your Child. Berkeley, California: Ulysses Press.

AutismOntario (2002). Navigating the Special Education System in Ontario: A Handbook for Parents of Children with Autism Spectrum Disorders. Toronto: Autism Society Ontario.

AutismOntario (2003). Children Diagnosed with Autism: What to Expect and Where to Get Help. Toronto: Autism Society Ontario.

AutismOntario (2006). Living with ASD: Adolescence and Beyond. Toronto: Autism Society Ontario.

Bandura, A. and Walters, R.H. (1963). Social learning and personality development. New York: Holt, Rinehart, & Winston.

Barbera, M. and Rasmussen, T. (2007). The Verbal Behavior Approach: How to Teach Children with Autism and Related Disorders. London and Philadelphia: Jessica Kingsley Publishers.

Betts & Betts. (2006). Yoga for Children with Autism Spectrum Disorders. London and Philadelphia: Jessica Kingsley Publishers.

Binder, Haughton and Bateman (2002). Fluency: Achieving True Mastery in the Learning Process. Professional Papers in Special Education. University of Virginia Curry School of Special Education (http://curry.edschool.virginia.edu/go/specialed/papers).

Cahill, D. and Cahill, M. (1989, 1991, 2003). The Goal Mine: Nuggets of Learning and Objectives for Exceptional Children, 5th edition. Fort Union, Virginia: iep publishing.

Carbone, V. The Verbal Behavior Approach to Teaching Children with Autism - a 7 CD set of videos

Cipano, E. And Schock, K.M. (2007). Functional Behavioral Assessment, Diagnosis, and Treatment. New York: Springer.

Cumpata, J. And Fell, S. (2010). A QUEST for Social Skills for Students with Autism or Asperger's. Arlington, Texas: Future Horizons.

Delaney, T. (2009). 101 Games and Activities with Autism, Asperger's, and Sensory Processing Disorders. New York: McGraw-Hill.

Ferber, R. (1985). Solve Your Child's Sleep Problems. New York: Simon and Schuster.

Fouse, B. (1999). Creating a "Win-Win IEP" for Students with Autism 2nd Edition. Arlington, Texas: Future Horizons.

Freeman, S.K. (2007). The Complete Guide to Autism Treatments: A parent's handbook: make sure your child gets what works! Langley, BC: SKF Books.

Freeman, S. and Dake, L. (1996, 1997). Teach Me Language: A language manual for children with autism, Asperger's syndrome and related developmental disorders. Langley, BC: SKF Books.

Gillingham, G.I. (2000). Autism: A New Understanding! Solving the Mystery of Autism, Asperger's and PDD-NOS. Edmonton, AB: Tacit Publishing.

Glasberg, B. (2006). Functional Behavioral Assessment for People with Autism: Making Sense of Seemingly Senseless Behavior. Bethesda, MD: Woodbine House.

Green, J.L. (2007). Technology for Communication and Cognitive Treatment: The Clinician's Guide. Potomac, MA: Innovative Speech Therapy.

Greenspan, S.I., DeGangi, G. And Wieder, S. (2001). The Functional Emotional Assessment Scale (FEAS) for Infancy and Early Childhood:

Clinical and Research Applications. Bethesda, MA: Interdisciplinary Council on Developmental and Learning Disorders.

Griffin, S. and Sandler, D. (2010). Motivate to Communicate: 300 Games and Activities for Your Child with Autism. London and Philadelphia: Jessica Kingsley Publishers.

Gutstein, S.E. (2009). The RDI Book. Houston, Texas: Connections Center Publishing.

Gutstein, S.E. and Sheely, R.K. (2002). Relationship Development Intervention with Young Children. London and Philadelphia: Jessica Kingsley Publishers.

Gutstein, S.E. and Sheely, R.K. (2002). Relationship Development Intervention with Children, Adolescents and Adults. London and Philadelphia: Jessica Kingsley Publishers.

Halfman, P. (2001). 100% Language: Activities for Language Comprehension. East Moline, IL: LinguiSystems

Hamilton, L. (2000). Facing Autism: Giving Parents Reasons for Hope and Guidance for Help. Colorado Springs, CO: WaterBrook Press.

HELP for Preschoolers Checklist: Ages 3 – 6 years (1995-2004) and Revised HELP Checklist: Birth to Three Years. (1984-2004). Palo Alto, CA: VORT Corporation.

Hoskins, B. (1996). Conversations: A Framework for Language Interventions. Eau Claire, WI: Thinking Publications.

Johnson-Martin, N.M., Hacker, B.J., and Attermeier, S.M. (2004). The Carolina Curriculum for Preschoolers with Special Needs, 2nd edition. Baltimore, MD: Paul Brookes Publishing.

Kluth, P. (2009). The Autism Checklist: A Practical Reference for Parents and Teachers. San Francisco, CA: Jossey-Bass.

Kluth, R. (2003). You're Going to Love This Kid! Teaching Students with Autism in the Inclusive Classroom. Baltimore, MA: Paul H. Brookes Publishing Co.

Kranowitz, C.S. (1998). The Out-of-Sync Child: Recognizing and Coping with Sensory Integration Dysfunction. New York: Berkley

Kranowitz, C.S. (2003). The Out-of-Sync Child Has Fun: Activities for Kids with Sensory Integration Dysfunction. New York: Berkley

Lansky, V. (1993). Games Babies Play: From Birth to Twelve Months. Minnetonka, MN: Book Peddlers.

Leaf, R., and McEachin, J., editors. (1999). A Work in Progress: Behavior Management Strategies and a Curriculum for Intensive Behavioral Treatment of Autism. New York: DRL Books.

Leaf, R., McEachin, J. and Taubman, M.(2008). Sense and Nonsense in the Behavioral Treatment of Autism: It Has to Be Said. New York: DRL Books.

Leaf, R., Taubman, M. and McEachin, J. (2008). It's Time for School! Building Quality ABA Educational Programs for Students with Autism Spectrum Disorders. New York: DRL Books.

Lear, K. (2004)' Help Us Learn: A Self-paced Training Program for ABA (The Training Manual and Program Manager's Guide). Toronto, ON: Help Us Learn.

Lehman, J.F. and Klaw, R. (2003/2006). From Goals to Data and Back Again: Adding Backbone to Developmental Intervention for Children with Autism. London and Philadelphia: Jessica Kingsley Publishers.

Lockshin, S.B., Gillis, J.M., and Romanczyk, R.G. (2005). Helping Your Child with Autism Spectrum Disorder: A Step-by-Step Workbook for Families. Oakland, CA: New Harbinger Publications.

Lovaas, O.I. (2003). Teaching Individuals with Developmental Delays: Basic Intervention Techniques. Austin, Texas: Pro-Ed.

Luckevich, D. 2004). Language Targets to Teach a Child to Communicate: A Resource to Manage Language Instruction. Issaquah, WA: Talking Words.

Mariposa School's Employee Training Manual, which may be downloaded for free from www.mariposaschool.org

Maurice, C. (1993). Let Me Hear Your Voice: A Family's Triumph Over Autism. New York: Fawcett Columbine (Ballantine Books).

Maurice, C. (editor) with Green & Luce. (1996). Behavioral Intervention for Young Children with Autism: A Manual for Parents and Professionals. Austin, TX: Pro-Ed.

Maurice, C., Green, G. and Foxx, R.M. editors (2001). Making a Difference: Behavioral Intervention for Autism. Austin, TX: Pro-Ed.

McAfee, J. (2002). Navigating the Social World. Arlington, TX: Future Horizons.

McKinnon, K. and Krempa, J. (2002). Social Skills Solutions: A Hands-on Manual for Teaching Social Skills to Children with Autism. New York, NY: DRL Books.

Partington, J. (2006). The Assessment of Basic Language and Learning Skills (The ABLLS-R). Pleasant Hill, CA: Behavior Analysts.

Pennypacker, H.S., Gutierrez, A. and Lindsley, O.R. (2003). Handbook of the Standard Celeration Chart, Deluxe Edition. Concord, MA: Cambridge Center for Behavioral Studies.
http://www.behavior.org/

Prizant, B.M., Wetherby, A.M., Rubin, E., Laurent, A.C., and Rydell, P.J. (2006). The SCERTS Model: A Comprhensive Educational Approach for Children with Autism Spectrum Disorders, Volume 1: Assessment. Baltimore, MA: Paul H. Brookes Publishing Co.

Prizant, B.M., Wetherby, A.M., Rubin, E., Laurent, A.C., and Rydell, P.J. (2006). The SCERTS Model: A Comprhensive Educational Approach for Children with Autism Spectrum Disorders, Volume 2: Program Planning and intervention. Baltimore, MA: Paul H. Brookes Publishing Co.

Rogers, S.J. and Dawson, G. (2010) Early Start Denver Model for Young Children with Autism: Promoting Language, Learning, and Engagement. New York, NY: The Guilford Press.

Schaefer, C.E., Kelly-Zion, S., McCormick, J., and Ohnogi, A. (Eds), (2008). Play Therapy for Very Young Children. New York, NY: Jason Aronson.

Schramm, R. (2006). Educate Toward Recovery: Turning the Tables on Autism. www.lulu.com: books.

Sher, B. (2006). Attention Games: 101 Fun, Easy Games That Help Kids Learn to Focus. San Francisco: Jossey-Bass.

Sher, B. (2009). Early Intervention Games. San Francisco: Jossey-Bass.

Singer, D.G. and Singer, J.L. (2001). Make-Believe Games and Activities for Imaginative Play. Washington, DC: Magination Press.

Smith, M. (2001). Teaching Playskills to Children with Autistic Spectrum Disorder: A Practical Guide. New York: DRL Books.

Smith, K.A. and Gouze, K.R. (2004). The Sensory-Sensitive Child: Practical Solutions for Out of Bounds Behavior. Toronto: HarperCollins.

Solomon, Richard. The P.L.A.Y. Project Workshop Level 1: Play and Language for Autistic Youngsters. (DVD) Ann Arbor, MI: The P.L.A.Y. Project (www.playproject.org)

Sonders, S.A. (2003). Giggle Time: Establishing the Social Connection. Philadelphia, PA: Jessica Kingsley Publishers.

Sundberg, M. and Partington, J. (1998). Teaching Language to Children with Autism or Other Developmental Disabilities. Pleasant Hill, CA: Behavior Analysts, Inc.

Sundberg, M. (2008). VB-MAPP: Verbal Behavior Milestones Assessment and Placement Program. Concord, CA: AVB Press.

Sussman, F. (1999). More Than Words. Toronto: The Hanen Centre.

Ward, S. (2008) What You Need to Know about Motivation and Teaching Games. www.lulu.com: books.

Weiss & Harris. (2001). Reaching Out, Joining In: Teaching Social Skills to Young Children with Autism. Brentwood, MD: Woodbine House.

Wenig, M. (2003). YogaKids. New York, NY: Abrams, Harry N., Inc..

Winner, M.G. (2000). Inside Out: What Makes a Person with Social-Cognitive Deficits Tick? San Jose, CA: Michelle Garcia Winner.

Winner, M.G. (2002). Thinking About YOU Thinking About ME. San Jose, CA: Michelle Garcia Winner.

Yack, E., Sutton, S., and Aquilla, P. (1998). Building Bridges Through Sensory Integration. Weston, ON: Print Three, Syd and Ellen Lerer.

Miscellaneous Websites

www.binder-riha.com/measurement_ideas.pdf *and* www.binder-riha.com/publications.htm (see 2004 and 2004, April).

www.celeration.net

www.chartshare.net

www.ChristinaBurkABA.com particularly for the section on *Effective Teaching Procedures.*

www.fluency.org *and* www.fluency.org/MeasurementCounts_Links.html

www.icdl.com (download their Clinical Practice Guidelines).

www.teachyourchildrenwell.ca/Home/mainpage.htm

www.teonor.com/ptdocs

A how-to-chart manual by Rick Kubina can be found at http://www.precisionteachingresource.net/chartoverview.pdf

and one by Carl Binder at http://www.binder-riha.com/Binder_ISPI2004_Charting.pdf

John Eshleman at members.aol.com/standardcharter/learnpix.html

home.wi.rr.com/penzky/pt.htm

members.aol.com/standardcharter

psych.athabascau.ca/html/387/OpenModules/Lindsley

seahorse.mma.edu/~sarna/index.html *and* seahorse.mma.edu/~sarna/sprints.html

About the Author

Reg Reynolds, Ph.D., C. Psych. is a graduate of the Clinical Psychology program at the University of Waterloo. He has been a psychologist for more that fifty years. During his career, he has functioned as a counsellor and psychotherapist for individuals, couples, and groups; as Chief Psychologist at the Ontario Correctional Institute, the Vanier Centre for Women, and the Oakville Reception and Assessment Centre (for juveniles admitted to training school); as a consultant regarding the assessment and treatment of sex offenders; as a consultant regarding ethical issues; as Coordinating Psychologist for the Central Region of Ontario Ministry of the Solicitor General and Correctional Services; as a researcher; as a college lecturer; as an intern in, clinical member of, and board member of the Halton Centre for Childhood Sexual Abuse; as an intern, co-therapist and therapist in the treatment of spousal abuse; as a member of the Council of the College of Psychologists of Ontario, as a developer of biofeedback equipment and as a provider of biofeedback; as a student of education and special education; as a student of Applied Behavioural Analysis (ABA) and its application in the treatment of children with autism; as psychologist and Supervising Clinician in the Ontario Government's Intensive Behavioural Intervention program for children with autism; as an educator of parents of children with autism; and, more recently, as a clinical supervisor of ABA-based programs for children with autism.

His most enduring work interests have been providing psychotherapy, trying to learn and apply the new energy therapies, trying to understand and treat criminality, developing equipment and protocols for biofeedback/neurofeedback, traumatization and, most recently, the treatment of autism spectrum disorders. His current avocational interests include multifaith dialogue, spirituality and spiritual healing, and his family – his wife and her many talents (especially her artistic work), and his children and grandchildren. Some of these interests are reflected on his website: www.RegReynolds.ca

Made in the USA
Middletown, DE
14 December 2020

28230604R00061